# *Teaching English Language Learners Through the Arts*

## *A SUAVE Experience*

**Merryl Goldberg, Editor**

*California State University, San Marcos*

Boston • New York • San Francisco
Mexico City • Montreal • Toronto • London • Madrid • Munich • Paris
Hong Kong • Singapore • Tokyo • Cape Town • Sydney

**Series editor:** *Aurora Martínez Ramos*
**Editorial assistant:** *Katie Freddoso*
**Senior marketing manager:** *Elizabeth Fogarty*
**Composition and prepress buyer:** *Linda Cox*
**Manufacturing buyer:** *Andrew Turso*
**Cover designer:** *Joel Gendron*
**Editorial-production administrator:** *Anna Socrates*
**Editorial-production service:** *Chestnut Hill Enterprises, Inc.*
**Electronic composition:** *Publishers' Design and Production Services, Inc.*

For related titles and support materials, visit our online catalog at www.ablongman.com.

**Library of Congress Cataloging-in-Publication Data**

Teaching English language learners through the arts : a SUAVE experience / Merryl
    Goldberg, editor.
        p. cm.
    Includes bibliographical references and index.
    ISBN 0-205-34383-X
    1. Linguistic minorities—Education (Elementary)—United States. 2. Children of
minorities—Education (Elementary)—United States. 3. Language arts—Correlation
with content subjects—United States. 4. Art in education—United States. 5. Multicultural education—United States. I. Goldberg, Merryl Ruth.

LC3725 .T44 2004
372.5—dc21

2003050213

All photos courtesy of Deborah Small.

Printed in the United States of America

10  9  8  7  6  5  4  3  2  1      07  06  05  04  03

*To the memory of my father, Jerry Goldberg, an incredible artist and teacher; and to all the students, artists, community members, friends, and family he touched in his seventy-two years of working wonder.*

# Contents

# *Preface*

Education, culture, and the arts are interwoven the same way fabric is made—they are essential parts of each other. Those of us who participate in the process of education need to have the necessary tools and opportunities to learn more not only about our own culture, but also about the cultures of others in order to fully understand who we are and where we are directing our steps in history.

Teaching English language learners (ELL) through the arts brings students and teachers alike into a magical and wonder-filled world. Those of us who teach students who are second language learners are very lucky indeed. We are privileged to enter into the lives of children who will grow up knowing at least two languages and at least two cultures. Wouldn't it be lovely if every child had this opportunity?

When I was growing up, my parents and grandparents used Yiddish as the language of secrets. It was spoken so that my brother and I could not understand what the adults were discussing. I remember my grandfather translating my English to Yiddish so that I could communicate with my great-grandmother, who did not speak English at all. I remember asking my grandfather over and over to teach me Yiddish phrases. My grandfather, being a wonderfully humorous fellow, taught me such phrases as *tsibila cup* (onion head) and *hok nit kein chainik* (you really give me a headache; or literally, don't bang on a tea kettle). I also remember my grandmother's dismay when she found out what phrases my grandfather chose to teach me. These are wonderful memories, and they are related not only to learning a language, but also to a process of enculturation.

I am not a Yiddish speaker today, although I wish had learned more. I do feel proud, however, to have a family background rich in culture and language. If my wishes could come true, every child in the world would learn multiple languages and become familiar with multiple cultures.

This book highlights and describes the workings of an award-winning and well-researched program called SUAVE (Socios Unidos para Artes Via Educación—United Community for Arts in Education). In this program, many children are second language learners, and all children have exposure to cultures in addition to their own. Through the voices of teachers, researchers, artists, and administrators, the successful journey of learning through the arts in ELL and bilingual classrooms comes to life in meaningful and significant ways. The stories combine firsthand accounts with researchers' analysis, providing a unique balance of practice and reflection.

*Susana Isakson, Bilingual SUAVE teacher from Fallbrook High School, California, using the jarana, a Mexican string instrument. to teach language skills.*

The book delves into all aspects of classroom practice, as well as the professional development practices that support students' learning through the arts-based methods. Each chapter includes firsthand accounts of successful ways to teach mathematics, science, language arts, social studies, and the arts themselves in an arts-rich environment. Pairing teachers with artists to enhance learning in ELL and bilingual classrooms helps bring out the potential of all students. This book is about ongoing practice, and all the examples are from real classrooms. The chapters are written from multiple perspectives, including teachers, artists, administrators, and researchers. Students' voices are included throughout.

It is the hope of all the authors that reading about our experiences will encourage you to try your adaptations of the ideas and lessons described. Keep in mind that you need not have art expertise in order to let your students learn through the arts. Children are natural artists, musicians, dramatists, puppeteers, storytellers, and dancers. Once you free them to learn and communicate their understandings through various art forms, your classroom will be opened to magic and wonder.

Children do not have the same filters as adults in terms of their willingness to play with art forms. Giving them the opportunity to work with the arts opens many avenues to them and to you as their teacher. You will see different identities and abilities, and you will see opportunities to connect in meaningful ways to the children as well as to the curriculum. If you are the least bit hesitant, try an arts activity. Your risk will pay off as soon as you see the children coming alive with excitement and energy. Unleash their imaginations, and you too will become enchanted by how exciting teaching and learning can become.

# With Thanks

So many people participate in the development and making of a book. All of the authors deserve special kudos for their passion, work, and willingness to contribute to this book. Many of the teachers and administrators have had little experience writing for books, but they nonetheless jumped fearlessly and enthusiastically into this project. Of course, none of it would be possible if it weren't for the children, teachers, and artists whose commitment to learning and creativity shine through their everyday activities, even in the midst of pressures imposed by frameworks and testing. I am lucky to be involved with such creative, imaginative, and dedicated people throughout my day.

The artists to whom I am deeply indebted include Donna Marie Cory, Mindy Donner, Kim Emerson, Eduardo Garcia, Kathryn Horn, Roxanne Kilbourne, Christina Mountari, Eduardo Parra, Abel Silvas, Robert Tod, Patti Christensen, and Berta Villaescusa. Another thanks to artist Eduardo Parra and to Corie Rose (a Bilingual Coordinator and teacher) for developing and sharing the fabric metaphor that opens this book. The teachers and children with whom I work are too numerous to mention individually; they represent the communities of Escondido, San Marcos, Valley Center, San Pasqual, Fallbrook, and Oceanside, California. Thanks also to the staff at the California Center for the Arts in Escondido, Peggy O'Neil, SUAVE coordinator, and Natasha Bonilla-Martinez, Director of Education and Visual Arts.

The Spencer and MacArthur Foundations funded a three-year research project on SUAVE through their special program of research related to professional development. Victoria Jacobs and Tom Bennett were an incredible research team and provided wonderful analysis throughout the project. Laura Wendling was on our team in the beginning, and her insights shaped much of the research as well. Much of what is reported in this book relates to that research. Their support, along with the support of the California Arts Council, the Fulbright-Hays Program, the California Department of Education, and many other granting agencies, has made it possible for thousands of students to receive learning experiences related to the arts. I am deeply grateful to all these institutions.

Thanks also to my colleagues in the Visual and Performing Arts Department at California State University San Marcos, especially David Avalos who headed SUAVE while I was on sabbatical and always has insights that prove to be great not only for the program but also for kids. Thanks to Lani Woods, support staff. And thanks to Deborah Small; she and my daughter Lili are two very influential individuals in my life—from gardening and birding to art and politics, all the while exploring the wonders of learning and knowing how they all fit together. Deborah's remarkable images of SUAVE participants appear throughout the book. Thanks also to my family and friends, a wonderfully eclectic and supportive group (Mom, Mark, Ron, Sid, Tomé, Ranjeeta, Jayant, Marie, Bonnie, Gunnar, Bill, and Dana, to name but a few). I would also like to recognize a group of folks and supporters who are involved in the creation of Center ARTES (Art, Research, Teaching, Education, and Schools) and who make dreams a possibility: Bonnie

Biggs, Rosita Botto-Hieb, Fran Chadwick, Greg Evans, Ruth Mangrum, Jamie Nelson, Jan O'Hara, John Santuccio, Laura Wendling, and Pat Worden.

Aurora Martinez, editor, and Beth Slater and Katie Freddoso, both editorial assistants, are three folks who know how to make things happen. Thanks to the copyeditor Sybil Sosin and the production editor Myrna Breskin at Chestnut Hill. I am fortunate to have worked with them as we moved through this project. I am also indebted to the individuals who so wonderfully reviewed this manuscript: Karima Benremouga, University of Houston; Gina Mikel Petrie, Washington State University; and Sharon Ulanoff, California State University, Los Angeles. No doubt they will notice their suggestions in this version.

# 1

# *Arts Ain't Fluff*

## Merryl Goldberg

*Front to back: Lili Goldberg, Merryl Goldberg, Elizabeth Covina, Eduardo Parra, and Lara Shumer creating a mural.*

*KEY CONCEPTS*
- ELL: Arriving in a new world
- Identity
- Respect for language and culture
- Art as a methodology for learning
- The role of wonder and passion in learning
- Teacher as a role model

| *El Mundo* | *The World* |
|---|---|
| *Al llegar a otro mundo,* | *To arrive in another world* |
| *Es como caer en un* | *is like falling into a* |
| *Hoyo negro todo sin* | *black hole all without* |
| *Color y sin risas.* | *Color and without laughter.* |
| | |
| *Es como buscar,* | *It's like looking* |
| *Algo que no se* | *for something you* |
| *Te ha perdido y que* | *have not lost and* |
| *Nunca podrás* | *you will never find.* |
| *Encontralo.* | |
| | |
| *Cada día se va* | *Every day passes* |
| *Y ni me doy cuenta,* | *and I can hardly account* |
| *Como se va. Tal vez* | *for it. Perhaps* |
| *Se lo lleva el viento,* | *the wind takes it,* |
| *Tal vez no.* | *perhaps not.* |

Piero Mercanti, seventh grade, translated by Maria Marrero, quoted in Steinbergh, 1991. Reprinted with permission.

As Piero so poignantly expresses, second language learners arrive not only to new languages, but also to new worlds. They arrive on the wishes and dreams of their families. For some children the transition is smooth and exciting. For some the transition is filled with a sense of loss in addition to newness. As we work with English language learners it is truly important to understand that these children live in multiple worlds made up of a past, the present, and a future. The past, especially for older children, is more than a collection of memories; it is how they have lived and what they know of the world. In the process of learning a new language, they will begin to reside in at least two worlds.

Eva Hoffman, a *New York Times* book reviewer who wrote about her own life in *Lost in Translation: A Life in a New World* (1989), arrived in the United States from Cracow, Poland, as a child of thirteen. She had a similar feeling to that of Piero. Her book begins:

> It is April 1959, I'm standing at the railing of the Batory's upper deck, and I feel that my life is ending. I'm looking out at the crowd that has gathered on the shore to see the ship's departure from Gdynia—a crowd that, all of a sudden, is irrevocably on the other side—and I want to break out, run back, run toward the familiar excitement, the waving hands, the exclamations. We can't be leaving this all behind—but we are. I am thirteen years old, and we are emigrating. It's a notion of such crushing, definitive finality that to me it might as well mean the end of the world. (p. 3)

Both Piero and Eva use very strong terms to describe the sense of loss and the heartfelt sadness of embarking on the road (or ocean) to a new world. As teachers, it is vitally important to recognize and respect that students like Piero, Eva, and the many others mentioned throughout the book have identities that no doubt revolve around their amazing and sometimes very difficult entry into a new world of language and culture.

A teacher can start creating bridges by first recognizing the fundamentally important role of a child's identity. As Jim Cummins (2000) writes, "Students' identities are affirmed and academic achievement promoted when teachers express respect for language and cultural knowledge that students bring to the classroom and when the instruction is focused on helping students generate new knowledge, create literature and art, and act on the realities that affect their lives" (p. 34).

## Theoretical Considerations

I teach a class at my university called learning through the arts. It is a required course for students who are in a multiple subject teaching credential program. In this class we discuss and then do activities relating to how to teach language arts, social studies, science, and mathematics with art and through the arts. For example, we explore the use of art prints to identify shapes; we listen to songs from periods in history to study social studies; we write poems based on headlines from a newspaper to encourage reading and writing; and we draw from nature in order to better understand it.

There are many ways in which the arts can be critical to English language learners (ELL). As the reader will see throughout the book, the arts give ELL students a viable and creative way to communicate understandings without always having to use or rely on verbal language. For example, a child who might not feel comfortable or be quite able to tell about the life cycle of a butterfly, but who understands it, might be able to draw it or act it out. Thus, through the arts, language barriers and ways to communicate about content can be bridged.

Some art forms explicitly promote the use of language. For example, when students write poetry on science or mathematics or create scripts for puppet shows depicting periods of history, the arts can be a path for language development and can support language growth. In some of my own research (Goldberg, 2000), poetry has shown to be highly effective in not only encouraging language development, but also inspiring an interest in reading. After writing original poems, students were motivated to read poems in the library to see how "other poets" created poems.

Arts can be a methodology for assessing students' understandings or motivating them to engage with subject matter. Art activities often inspire and motivate children to learn. They become excited by the work and have a chance to practice imagination. Teachers who work with second language learners in the SUAVE program (which is described fully in Chapter 2) consistently report that arts integration can be the key in enabling students to participate and shine.

Through creating an artwork or acting out a concept such as the movement of the planets, students show us their understandings, perhaps before they can articulate them in the English language. As will be shown throughout the book, the arts give rise to alternative and effective ways to assess students' understanding of content matter. This ability to show understandings can be a jumping-off point for discussing the content. It can also let ELL students share and even show off, whereas they would hesitate if their only option were verbal language.

The arts enable teachers to see more of the child, and thus assess the child's understandings more authentically. For example:

- "In many ways it goes beyond language, which can be challenging for so many students. Those students whose native language is not English, or English communication is verbally or written difficult for them [sic] . . . it levels the plane and everybody can bring something creative to the game and I like how it does that."
- "I feel it has offered [the students] a variety of ways to show me their understanding of concepts."
- "As we do more art in the classroom, I begin to see children differently because I see them do well when in other areas they did not seem to do so well. I see them more as valuable individuals because I am in contact with the *whole* person."
- "I like giving more options for more students to *shine,* especially those not very verbal or academic in the traditional sense."

Finally, the arts are a critical tool in bridging and respecting the many cultures that can be present in K–12 classrooms. Through engaging in arts activities and experiencing the arts of other cultures, students attain an understanding of each other as individuals and of each other's cultures. Activities in the arts can connect students through mime, performance, and appreciating individual creations such as drawings and sculptures.

While this book is intended to highlight the role arts can play in classrooms with second language learners, it is by no means a methodology for teaching English as a second language (ESL) nor a definitive methodology for teaching language skills. This would be quite a task; research reported by Jim Cummins (2000) shows that on average it "takes a minimum of about five years (and frequently much longer) for them to catch up to native speakers in academic aspects of language" (p. 34). In addition, a child's conversational ability might be quite different from his or her academic or literate ability. Therefore, while a child may be able to tell us or act out something, her or his ability to write or read could be lagging.

A child's literacy skill levels in his or her first language will also have a bearing on the child's ability to transfer knowledge to a second language (Cummins, 2000). According to Sandra Lee McKay, "the attainment of effective educational programs for English language learners requires long-term material and intellectual investment on the part of teachers, administrators, family and community" (McKay & Wong, 2000, p. 395). There are debates about what methods—submersion, pull-out, bilingual, or two-way bilingual programs—are most effective.

This book does not take a stance on a particular methodology. Instead, it posits that the arts, no matter what a school district decides in terms of a program, can help students learn a new language and can be a useful tool for their teachers to help them with their new language. Across the chapters, however, the reader will find a bias for respecting and retaining the child's first language and a philosophical stance that being multilingual is a wonderful attribute.

Among the many theories relating to second language acquisition, Steven Krashen's (1981) affective filter hypothesis is apropos to the role arts can play in language development. Krashen's hypothesis is that a low-anxiety learning environment is conducive to effectively learning language. In such an environment, the child is more likely to be motivated to use new language, and his or her self-confidence and self-esteem is likely to be encouraged. Working with arts often creates an environment of "can do." Students are drawn to the arts and motivated because they can use their imaginations freely and be creative without the limitations of language. Art creation can also be a springboard for language development. Thus, the arts can lead to success by building on what students can create on their own terms.

Scaffolding—another term found in second language acquisition theory—can be a useful tool in integrating the arts into the classroom that houses English language learners. Scaffolding is a process by which teachers support and assist learners so that they may move onto the next level of development in learning. Singing songs, acting out stories, and dramatizing poetry all can provide students with concrete ways to build upon language (Peregoy & Boyle, 2000) because they include repetition, or something familiar upon which the student can build.

## Who are Second Language Learners?

Children who are second language learners might arrive with family members escaping a repressive government; they might come as six year olds from Chinese, Russian, Mexican, Romanian, or other orphanages; they might be children of visiting university professors; they might be children of migrant workers from Central America; or they might be joining other family members who are already starting new lives in a big city. Many children who speak other languages have grown up in the United States while speaking the languages of their families in their homes. All children, no matter what their entrance to a new language might be, come to their new language with a past and a history. All children also come with a capacity to learn and wonder.

According to Shirley Brice Heath (1986), whether students are immigrants or native born, they bring their own cultures to the enterprise of schooling. Furthermore, Peregoy and Boyle (2000, p. 3) write that "each group contributes to the rich tapestry of languages and cultures that form the basic fabric of the United States." Thus, knowing our students is key to being able to reach them in the classroom. "The starting point for understanding why students choose to engage academically or, alternately withdraw from academic efforts," according to Cummins (2000), "is to acknowledge that *human relationships are at the heart of schooling*." He continues that "all of us know this from our own schooling experiences. If we felt that a teacher believed in us and cared for us then we put forth much more effort than if we felt that she or he did not like us or considered us not very capable (p. 40)."

I remember visiting my grandmother, herself an immigrant fluent in Yiddish as well as English, at her home just outside of Boston, Massachusetts. When I was in college, the elementary school next door was going through an amazing transformation. There had been an influx of Cambodian students, and the school was trying to develop tools to teach language and literacy skills.

What the school's staff realized first, however, was that they needed to know more about the Cambodian language, students, and culture before they could begin developing methods for teaching the new students. Consequently, the staff worked with the community, and everyone was given workshops in language and customs, to try to understand each other before attempting to teach the new students. That made a profound impression on me. I was struck with the simplicity of the notion—learn about each other before attempting to teach one another.

## The Capacity to Learn and Wonder

"If I had influence with the good fairy who is supposed to preside over the christening of all children," writes Rachel Carson (1965/1998), "I should ask that her gift to each child in the world be a sense of wonder so indestructible that it would last throughout life" (pp. 42–43). Children are natural wonderers. Their worlds are filled with newness, and as teachers we are in the unique position of keeping that wonder central to their lives. Even the children who have come to us from seemingly hopeless situations caused by politics or poverty have not lost the instinct of wonder, though it might need to be rekindled. Children also have passions, and uncovering those passions gives us insights into the children and what might motivate them to learn.

When Rachel Carson wrote about wonder, she was talking to her readers (especially parents) as a naturalist. Other naturalists also discuss wonder as it relates to children. I find this to be quite apropos to thinking about all learners and what is at the core of knowledge. Sue Halpern (2001) gets to the crux of this issue by asking, "How do people know what they know?" She writes of science and continues, "The world presents itself: the sky is blue, the birds are singing. Our senses are an open window. . . . Science, like any belief, starts with wonder, and wonder starts with a question" (p. 199). She relates wonder to passion and the irrational in a thought provoking excerpt:

> All these years later, I hardly remembered the difference between an igneous and a metamorphic rock. What I did remember was the single-mindedness with which I had picked through the woods behind my house, and the pure joy of finding some-

thing valuable enough to hold on to. It seemed reasonable to call this passion, and to think of myself—and everyone else—as a collection of passions. What this suggests is that it is not simply our ability to think, to be rational, that distinguishes humans from other species, but our ability to be *irrational*—to put stones in our pockets because we think they are beautiful. (pp. 8–9)

What I love about this excerpt is the idea of people as "a collection of passions." I think this is a wonderful way to approach children in our classrooms. Each and every child holds his or her own collection of passions. If as teachers we can tap into and find out what the passions are, we will have a better chance to connect and reach each child. Of course, with English language learners this becomes a bit more of a challenge because students might not be able to tell us about their passions. In this case, art can be an important tool for both teachers (in uncovering passions) and students (in expressing passions).

## The Importance of Teacher as Role Model

Teachers have a unique role in keeping wonder and passion alive in children's lives. Teachers are also role models for students. As teachers, parents, guardians, and important adults in children's lives, we influence in many ways how children think and what they do. We are role models in our words, actions, and views of others and the world. One of the best descriptions of this I have come across recently is the song "Children Will Listen" by Steven Sondheim from the musical *Into the Woods*. In this song, the listener is cautioned to be careful of the things that are said, because children will hear them. Be careful of things you do, because children will observe them. Children always listen and observe. Be careful with your thoughts and actions, for you are your children's role model.

The song highlights the importance of our words, actions, and responses to children. Even when we might think we are not teaching, we are. The way we treat children in our classes teaches them about how people treat each other. If we neglect to honor a child's first culture and language, we are teaching that his or her past is insignificant. Though that might not be what a teacher's attitude really is, the actions are what is really being taught. Consequently, if we honor children's first languages and cultures in meaningful ways, we are teaching them that their pasts are important and significant.

I remember being in middle school and singing in the chorus. We prepared for a Christmas concert in December. I am Jewish. To this day I remember feeling uncomfortable singing Christmas carols, and feeling as if my culture somehow didn't matter. I also didn't feel comfortable enough to speak up and ask if we could sing a Hanukah song, or if I could be excused from singing songs about Jesus. What was being taught to me through role modeling was that my culture was not as important as the dominant culture. Now, I am sure that my teachers were respectful of my religion and culture, yet for some reason this didn't play into how the music for a particular concert was chosen.

In visiting schools today, I am very aware of choices that can be made in situations like a holiday concert. Two schools I visited recently created a holiday program for December that was called "Holidays around Our Community and Our World." In these two schools, the teachers have made an effort to not only find about the traditions of their students, but also to add traditions from cultures not represented by their students. In this case, what is being taught through modeling is that there is a wide variety of holiday traditions both in the United States and around the world, that it is important to be aware of multiple traditions, and that traditions come in a variety of languages.

As role models, if we take risks in our teaching and in the way we present subject matter (or question subject matter), we are teaching our students that it is good to take risks. If we incorporate the arts as a language for learning, we are teaching them that the arts are valuable ways to express themselves. If we follow our own passions and share them with our students, we are teaching our students the joy of exploring and embracing passion. Our actions are very important; they represent something more than decisions about pedagogy.

Many ELL students who enter classrooms are nervous about taking risks with language. Vicki Rosenberg, who teaches in southern California, talks about some of her students who spoke no English when they first came to class. One boy was extremely vivacious in Spanish. On the playground using his Spanish he was really talkative, but in the classroom he was very, very reluctant to use English.

Vicki's class was creating puppet shows with the encouragement of her SUAVE coach, an artist who was helping her integrate the arts throughout the curriculum. This boy was quite excited about the puppet show; however, when it came time to perform, he was absent from school. As it turned out, he was embarrassed about his inability to use English and his accent—embarrassed enough to stay at home rather than come to school. Throughout the year, the class created and performed more and more puppet shows and even videotaped them. Eventually, this boy became more involved. As it turned out, Vicki said, "he was a wonderful performer, but it was just hidden under all this fear of language."

> Once he found out what he could do it gave him the opportunity to build up his confidence zone. I would never have thought that it could have had such a drastic effect. He is really one of the greatest [kids and performers].

Vicki had another student she described as extremely shy and stubborn. She wouldn't answer questions on oral tests if a stranger was giving the test. "She just sits like a stone and won't say anything." Her comfort zone is with Vicki, but when a stranger or the principal comes into the room she won't speak at all. Yet, when Vicki introduced puppetry into the curriculum, this child came completely alive. In fact, out of all the parts in the puppetry plays, she chose to be a narrator, the longest speaking part! The puppetry became a motivating force in the child's willingness to participate in oral language. Vicki's students were engaged in uncovering passions, building joy and wonder, and they were gaining confidence in themselves. Vicki reflected on the experiences with the two children in this way:

> Those moments are really worth it when you stop and see the growth that they have made. Probably the most unique thing is the change in their self-esteem. Maybe the kids academically are not quite at grade level yet, but they have an 'I can' attitude when they walk out of the door, and they value themselves and something they have done in the classroom. Those are magical moments.

Like all students, children who are learning another language learn in many ways. Children can be visually oriented, kinesthetic, aural, or logico-mathematical thinkers. While it is good pedagogical practice to keep open all venues for students, it is especially important to do so with second language learners who have the additional burden of expressing themselves in a new language. Imagine the frustration that can occur when a student clearly understands a concept or has a passion to share but cannot communicate it because of a limited vocabulary. The challenge here is not to simply open venues to students to express their understandings, but to offer openings to teachers to see what their students know.

Pat Griffith teaches elementary school in Escondido, California, about fifty miles north of the border with Tijuana, Mexico. She talks about her class and the way drawing can foster the building of vocabulary:

> In this class, a lot of the kids that are very artistic are sort of limited in vocabulary. They can draw a picture that is much more complex but they can't talk about it. Then, [they] use the picture as a basis for using more vocabulary. Since vocabulary is such a part of how we judge people and evaluate people, if you come from a situation where there is not extensive vocabulary in the house or a different language, then a really important part of school is vocabulary. I believe that if you integrate art in any subject then there is better chance that the subject will be retained and used by the child.

As teachers learn what their students are capable of and the ways in which they can and love to learn, the teachers have many more opportunities to work with their students. In other words, the arts can open windows to teachers that offer insights into not only what students know, but also how they know it. This might not happen in an instant; it might take time.

Dale Murphy teaches fifth graders, also in Escondido. She describes how learning can take time and how the arts can level the playing field for all students. An observer came to her room to watch a lesson on comparing and contrasting. After the lesson, Dale said to the observer:

Maybe you don't know that in this class I have two RSP (Resource Specialist) kids, I have a GATE (Gifted and Talented Education) student, I have twenty-three second language learners, and I have two non-English proficient learners. But you didn't know that. When you look at an art lesson then you think they are all on an equal playing field. Art does take time but doesn't learning? You want to invest the time. If you really want the students to know what you are trying to teach them and truly understand the concepts then you need to let them get into it. To me this is worth the time.

Dale has important points to make. By enabling her students to work through this exercise by means of a visual arts activity, she made it virtually impossible to know who among the students was proficient or nonproficient in English language skills. The "playing field," as she describes it, was leveled. All of the students could be successful. This, as she pointed out, can take time. Time, however, is not a dirty word! Most learning and the development of new ideas happen over long periods of time. It is difficult at best to balance the demands of standards, frameworks, and curriculum with time in school settings. However, it is important to remind ourselves that learning can and does take time and to keep creating those openings for taking the time to learn.

## What Is Art?

Art is an attitude and way of being in the world. It is also a series of products—painting, sculptures, songs, dances, poems, dramas, performances. Artists (like children) rarely see the world as either/or. Through viewing or creating art, children can explore ideas and feelings in an unrestricted and creative manner. In science in the fourth grade, for example, a teacher might encourage her students to express a concept such as metamorphosis through poetry or movement. Words in an oral or written report might be difficult for an ELL student, while poetry enables the same student to apply words without the fear of using grammar or syntax incorrectly. Movement might allow the student to freely express understandings that are hidden beneath the self-consciousness of mispronouncing a word.

It is not unusual for people to ask, "What is art?" Nelson Goodman, a Harvard philosopher, considered a dilemma inherent in this question. "What is art?" implies a judgment on finished works of art. Goodman offered another question, "When is art?" In asking this question he pushed us to see art as a way of looking at the world rather than as a finished product. As did Rachel Carson with her attention to nature, Goodman had a sense that if we would only stop and ponder, we might find ourselves noticing art in the least expected places. In fact, art is many things. Art can be objects: paintings on museum walls, sculptures in our living rooms, statues in the town park, murals on city buildings, drawings by children, Internet Web pages, and movie landscapes. Art is also a method of knowing and a language that provides both artists and audiences an opportunity to wonder, imagine, be passionate, be outraged, and question and reflect on our lives—a chance to see things that are or aren't there.

Many ELL students come from countries in which arts are more culturally interwoven in and important to everyday life than in the United States. One need not be an artist in order to act in the way an artist acts, or to create art. In fact, in many societies and cultures there isn't even a word for "art" with quite the same meaning as in the Western tradition of fine art. A fundamental aspect of "arting" is the ability to stop, notice, and ponder the ways in which creating and infusing art might serve your goals as a teacher.

Examining almost any art form lends insight into the fundamental role of arts in culture and knowledge. Angela Davis's *Blues Legacies and Black Feminism* (1998) speaks to this point. The book concerns itself with the genre of the blues tradition here in the United States, especially as it relates to women and feminism, and it informs our understanding of the role of arts in human experience, expression, and communication. Through her examination of the music and of what others have written about the music, Davis discusses blues and blues singers as dynamic spokespersons, interpreters of dreams, revealers of harsh realities, and tragicomedies of the black experience in the first three decades of the twentieth century. She eloquently reminds the reader that traditions, including the multiple African American feminist traditions, "are not only written, they are oral, and that these oralities reveal not only rewrought African cultural traces, but also the genius with which former slaves forged new traditions that simultaneously contested the slave past and preserved some of the rich cultural products of slavery" (p. xix).

We need to keep in mind that although schooling might tend to favor written traditions, our multiple cultures and histories value oral and other traditions, and these traditions might inform our ways of teaching and being in this world. They need not be entirely separate from each other. The oral tradition of the blues might tempt a reluctant speaker, or for that matter rap and rapping might be a key to opening up an otherwise shy or quiet student. A reluctant speaker might love singing or rapping and excel in that area. As a teacher, you might encourage that oral tradition, then gently guide the child toward writing her or his lyrics down on paper or reading lyrics that others have composed. Perhaps you can even have the child present the lyrics of others to the class.

## Conclusion

Respect for who we are, where we've come from, and where we are going is at the core of creating a classroom that is conducive to learning and being human. Languages are at the very core of who we are and who we choose to be. We all live in multiple worlds and have multiple identities depending on which world we are in at any given time.

The arts are fundamental traditions and tools for all people in all cultures. They can be fantastically inviting and freeing for students as another language, one that unites rather than divides, through which an individual can find hope rather than despair. The arts can be a tool for unity in a classroom where words might be inadequate or inappropriate. Finally, the arts will bring life to the children and the subjects they connect.

## *References*

Carson, R. (1965/1998). *The sense of wonder*. New York: HarperCollins Publishers.

Cummins, J. (2000). *Language, power and pedagogy: Bilingual children in the crossfire*. Clevedon, England: Multilingual Matters Ltd.

Davis, A. (1998). *Blues legacies and black feminism*. New York: Vintage Books, a division of Random House, Inc.

Goldberg, M. (2000). *Arts and learning: An integrated approach to teaching and learning in multicultural and multilingual settings*, 2nd ed. New York: Longman.

Halpern, S. (2001). *Four wings and a prayer: Caught in the mystery of the monarch butterfly*. New York: Pantheon Books.

Heath, S. B. (1986). Sociocultural contexts of language development. In California State Department of Education (Ed.), *Beyond language: Social and cultural factors in schooling language minority students* (pp. 143–186). Los Angeles: Evaluation, Dissemination and Assessment Center, California State University.

Hoffman, E. (1989). *Lost in translation: A life in a new world*. New York: Penguin Books.

Krashen, S. (1981). Bilingual education and second language acquisition theory. In California State Department of Education (Ed.), *Schooling and language minority students: A theoretical framework*. Los Angeles: Evaluation, Dissemination and Assessment Center, California State University.

McKay, S. L., & Wong, S. C. (2000). *New immigrants in the United States*. Cambridge, UK.: Cambridge University Press.

Peregoy, S., & Boyle, O. (2000). *Reading, writing, and learning in ESL: A resource book for K–12 teachers*, 3d ed. New York: Addison Wesley Longman.

Steinbergh, J. (1991). To arrive in another world: Poetry, language development, and culture. *Harvard Educational Review* 61 (1).

Goodman, Nelson (1976). *Languages of Art*. Indianapolis/Cambridge: Hackett Publishing Co.

# 2

# The Professional Development Program: SUAVE

**Merryl Goldberg**

*July Rose, SUAVE arts coach.*

## KEY CONCEPTS

- Learning through the arts
- Learning about arts
- Professional development for teachers
- Art coaches in ELL classrooms
- In-service training
- Affective and cognitive beliefs

The work and practices presented throughout this book come from a program called SUAVE. SUAVE (Socios Unidos para Artes via Educación, or United Community for Arts in Education) is a volunteer professional development program in southern California that was developed in 1993 by Merryl Goldberg with local arts educators and arts center staff, and with input from local elementary teachers and principals. It was developed as a collaboration among the California Center for the Arts-Escondido, California State University San Marcos, and several local school districts (Goldberg & Bossenmeyer, 1998).

The community is just fifty miles north of the Mexican border. In the districts that SUAVE serves, the Latino student population is significant: 50.2 percent in Escondido, 45 percent in San Marcos, and 25.8 percent in Valley Center (data obtained through the California Department of Education). Most of the Latino students are of Mexican origin (although the county figures do not differentiate between various peoples of Hispanic origin). A goal and outcome of this project is to connect with culture and arts that represent and are important to the students in our service area, as well as develop ways to integrate the culture and arts in interdisciplinary learning.

The philosophy underlying the program is that teaching *through* the arts (in contrast to the more traditional teaching *about* the arts) can be a powerful pedagogical tool for teachers to help students both further their subject-matter understanding and be introduced to the arts themselves (ASCD Curriculum Update, 1998; Goldberg, 2001). It was created to meet the needs of multilingual and multicultural learning communities in southern California, but can certainly be applied to other areas where there are second language learners.

The work of SUAVE is carried out by a group of art specialists (coaches) who are skilled in teaching with and through the arts. They work in partnership with local public school teachers (as opposed to taking over classes) to help them approach all areas of the curriculum in more creative and interactive ways. This creative process of teaching and learning also allows teachers and students to have better access to and understanding of other cultures and contributes to creating individuals who are creative, critical, and analytical thinkers with better understanding of and deeper respect for themselves and others. In one of the school districts, SUAVE serves as the visual and performing arts curriculum for the district, and the arts coaches serve as the district's arts specialists. In some districts, the SUAVE arts specialists are supplemented by a few other arts coaches paid for through PTA funds.

One of the strategies SUAVE utilizes to make classroom learning a deeper and more complete and meaningful experience is exposure to the cultures of other nations. This strategy allows those involved in SUAVE to acknowledge the important role that each culture plays in this world and to contribute, expand, and enrich the learning process by integrating new experiences and learning from the cultural and educational exchange with other countries. For example, SUAVE teachers and art coaches received a Fulbright-Hays scholarship in 1999 to study puppetry in India. This experience resulted in a unique opportunity to learn about Indian culture, to interact and work with teachers and students from different regions of that country, and to expand their knowledge of using art techniques in education, which impacted the work that SUAVE is currently doing with teachers and students in the United States. In 2002 SUAVE received a second Fulbright-Hays scholarship that enabled twenty teachers and artists to travel to Veracruz, Mexico to study the music and dance of Mexico.

SUAVE currently involves a dozen full-time coaches and approximately two hundred teachers from over twenty schools across five districts as active participants. Over the years, we have reached over a thousand teachers, many of whom continue to be active in SUAVE through participation in in-service days and workshops. Almost all the teachers have ELL students in their classrooms. When we began, the districts all had bilingual classrooms, and SUAVE was present in bilingual classrooms. However, as a result of legislation to ban bilingual education, most students are now in integrated classrooms. In any case, an important element of SUAVE is focusing on teachers of ELL students.

For the first two years of participation, a school site selects ten teachers to participate in in-services and weekly coaching sessions. The goal at the end of two years is for teachers to have gained the ability and desire to continue teaching through the arts. After two years, teachers no longer have a coach in their classrooms weekly, yet they are still provided with opportunities to participate in after-school workshops, attend in-services, and work with coaches in their classrooms.

## Weekly Coaching

The core of SUAVE is its coaching component, whereby a professional artist (the coach) visits each teacher's classroom one hour per week for two years. The coaches are supported through weekly meetings with the program director (fully described in Chapter 10). SUAVE is designed so that ten teachers per school site work with the same coach. The coaches rotate yearly, so that each teacher has an opportunity to work with two coaches over the two years. The coaches do not try to implement a set of preplanned art activities. Rather, their task is to collaborate with teachers to further the teachers' curriculum objectives and professional development goals.

In contrast to a traditional coaching model in which the coach would be the "expert" and the teacher a "novice," SUAVE views teachers as an integral part of successful classroom coaching. While coaches bring professional knowledge about the arts (e.g., techniques, creativity, multiple modes of communication, and a curiosity for exploring the world), teachers bring professional knowledge about teaching and the students in their classrooms (e.g., curriculum knowledge, classroom management skills, age-appropriate expectations, and a rapport with specific students). These two then collaborate to design lessons that teach curriculum through the arts. The lessons are customized for a particular topic and particular students (rather than being a prescribed curriculum). They are also designed to be appropriate for the comfort level and ability level of the teacher and coach involved. This collaboration often creates instruction that is substantially better than either feels capable of producing alone (Bennett et al., 1999).

## In-Services

SUAVE provides four to five full-day in-services per year for all participating teachers. During these in-services, teachers share curriculum, attend performances, learn arts-based activities from local and visiting artists, and have the opportunity to take workshops from scheduled performers. For example, over the years teachers have had the opportunity to meet and work with the Shakespeare Company, dancer Bella Lewitsky, Ballet Hispanico, and Marcel Marceau.

Over the many years of SUAVE, we have documented and researched various aspects of the program. For the purposes of this book, let me highlight five areas that are of special interest.

- Documenting and describing the benefits and challenges of the relationship between artists and teachers
- Understanding the coaching relationship
- Identifying and describing key elements of a successful coaching relationship by documenting and describing the customized component of classroom-based coaching (rather than a prescribed program of activities)
- Documenting and describing the role and importance of sustained support for coaches
- Identifying and describing the factors that support sustained change for teachers

## Documenting and Describing the Benefits and Challenges of the Relationship between Artists and Teachers

When we began looking closely at SUAVE, one of our chief aims was to describe the benefits and challenges of what we originally called an "expert-expert" relationship between teachers and artists as they worked together on the methodology of teaching subject matter through arts-based means. We later changed the wording to a "professional-professional" relationship because participants defined themselves as professionals rather than experts. The pairing of artists and teachers is unique in the world of professional development. Outsiders are rarely brought into the world of education as professional developers for teachers.

As they interacted with each other, the participants (both artists and teachers) felt very much like they were inventors, creating new curricula all the time. In that sense, they did not feel like experts; in fact, the word *novice* perhaps better described their ability to create and adapt the curriculum. However, they did feel professional in their dealings with each other. Thus, the description "professional-professional" emerged, honoring the expertise that each partner brought to the professional development, but at the same time acknowledging the newness of the work together. We found that the fact that each relationship worked toward creating new curriculum (i.e., customized coaching) meant that participants often felt like learners rather than experts. Thus, we changed our description to "professional-professional," which felt comfortable to our participants.

Teachers in SUAVE have made shifts in affective and cognitive beliefs, especially with regard to how they view their students. They have also made changes to their instructional practices (see Bennett, Goldberg, & Jacobs, 1999). Teachers' beliefs have shifted in terms of recognizing how arts impact students' self-confidence and motivation to participate and take risks in class. Teachers have also recognized how teaching through the arts can impact their views of students' cognitive abilities. This has been especially true in terms of seeing "lower level students as academically more competent" as a result of enabling them to express their understandings through the arts (Bennett, Goldberg, & Jacobs, 1999). This suggests that perhaps lower-level students are not lower at all, but demonstrate competence in ways other than language.

Changes in teachers' instructional practices as they integrate the arts include

- Learning to engage students mentally and physically in the learning process
- Learning to provide students with opportunities to explore, investigate, and discover
- Learning to create new ways for students to represent their ideas and for teachers to assess students' understanding of the content
- Learning to be less inhibited in the classroom

Interestingly, we found the greatest benefits when learning occurred not only for the teacher (the main beneficiary of the professional development), but rather for all participants: teacher, artist, and students. Clearly, the nature of the program as an on-the-job professional development program adds to the success in the sense that the results of the teacher learning are tangible because they are measured against student learning.

There are challenges to the teacher-artist relationships. We highlight one extreme case in Chapter 11. While the program has been remarkably successful both in terms of teacher learning and teacher satisfaction, teacher-artist collaborations have not been without tensions. Victoria Jacobs (2000) describes two sources of tension. First, teachers typically work in a culture that supports autonomy and equality and thus are used to working in their own classrooms without contributions or critiques from others (Little, 1990; McClure, 1999). Similarly, when artists work in schools, they do so autonomously as specialists (Goldberg, 2001). Thus, given the unfamiliarity of teachers and artists meeting in collaboration, this professional development program forces them to negotiate what form the collaboration should take, and tensions often arise.

Second, collaborations with individuals outside of education require melding two professional worlds, each with its own goals, values, and typical practices. Teachers exist in a world of content standards, mandatory testing, and results-driven rewards and policies. These conditions encourage them to be time-conscious and objective-driven (McClure, 1999; Sparks & Hirsch, 1997). In contrast, artists value the artistic process, a process of creation that requires spontaneity and time for exploration (Bennett et al., 1999; Goldberg, 1997). Tensions often arise as the coaches try to help the teachers incorporate the artistic process into a curriculum that is already full.

Jacobs writes (2000, pp. 2–3) that two caveats are required in order to understand these tensions: First, the tensions did not occur in all teacher-coach collaborations or all lessons. Second, although tensions can create anxiety and frustration, all tensions should not be viewed as negative. In many cases, tensions can provide exceptional opportunities for growth, and research has suggested that a certain amount of uncertainty or difficulty is necessary for substantial teacher learning to occur (Ball & Cohen, 1999; Fullan, 1999; Fullan & Miles, 1992; Goldberg, Bennett, & Jacobs, 1999; Thompson & Zeuli, 1999). Thus, Jacobs concludes by identifying structural components of the SUAVE program that seem to have mitigated many of the potentially negative effects of these tensions and instead have turned them into opportunities for teacher learning. Those structural components include the sustained nature of the coaching (two years), the community support throughout (in schools and at in-services), and the customized nature of the program. These support mechanisms serve as safety nets and allow the participants to work through tensions rather than be hampered by them.

## Understanding the Coaching Relationship

The program's label for artists in the classroom is "coach." The artists, however, do not act like typical coaches, let's say sports coaches. Instead they are more typical of the origin of the word "coach," which as described in the Oxford dictionary, refers to coach as something that transports something or someone, for example a stagecoach. The SUAVE coach moves or conveys a teacher from point A to point B, and is the vehicle, therefore along for the ride. The coach—with the teacher being conveyed—travel together. The teacher has a voice in where the coach is going and how it gets there (Goldberg, Bennett, & Jacobs, 1999; Goldberg, 1998).

As we progressed with our research, we were interested in looking at how a relationship between an artist and a teacher can be beneficial to the professional development of a teacher, and ways in which it can be challenging or even limiting. Going into the study, we knew from program evaluations and preliminary studies that the participants generally found the relationships successful. The program was receiving very high marks not only from the participants, but also from school administrators, districts, and state and federal grantors (California Arts Council, California Department of Education, federal Title VII grants).

If one were to judge the program by the participant evaluations, one would be very happy. While it was true that most participants were extremely happy, they also were cognizant of the tenuous position of arts in the schools and acted in ways to ensure the program's continuation. In other words, praise for the program could mean its continuity. However, the enthusiastic program marks did not reflect the tension that would sometimes arise between artists and teachers due to the differences between artistic worlds and teaching worlds. Tension manifested itself, for example, in occasional clashes about the exploratory time that the artists valued versus the need to have a product, which teachers often felt obliged to deliver (see Bennett, 2000; Goldberg, Bennett, & Jacobs, 1999; Jacobs, 2000).

## Identifying and Describing Key Elements of a Successful Coaching Relationship

To successfully teach children content through the arts requires understanding the content, students, teaching, and the arts. The artist brings his or her knowledge of the arts, and the teacher brings his or her knowledge of the content, students, and teaching. In this type of professional-professional relationship, both teacher and artist assume the role of expert as well as learner. Therefore, the artist and teacher must work collaboratively and share their expertise to successfully teach children content through the arts. Teachers and artists primarily collaborate in two ways: planning lessons, and presenting lessons to students.

Although there is no set model for how the teacher and artist are to work together as a result of the customized process of collaboration, many similarities have emerged across relationships. For example, the teachers often identify the content to be taught through the arts based on academic objectives. Together, the teacher and coach then generate ideas on how they might teach the topics through the arts, taking into account the ELL learners as well the multiple learning styles that have emerged in the classroom. As we might expect, the artist generally brings forth the ideas related to the arts, and the teacher checks these ideas against his or her objectives. This is not to say that the teachers do not at times contribute ideas related to the arts, or that artists do not contribute ideas related to students or teaching. We have also found that the teachers contribute to the planning process by ensuring that the lessons will be appropriate for the age and ability level of the class. Once a general idea for how the lesson will be taught is agreed upon, the artist typically assumes responsibility for planning and preparing to teach the artistic component of the lesson, and the teacher assumes the role of organizing the lesson and bringing forward the academic objectives. We have found that as the teachers become more competent in integrating the arts into the curriculum, they often begin to assume greater responsibility for the arts component of the lessons.

Rather than creating lesson plans in advance, some teacher-artist teams create their lessons "on the spot" when the artist arrives in the classroom. Often the teacher will have a general idea of concept to be taught for that day's lesson. When the artist arrives in the classroom, the teacher and artist meet briefly to brainstorm ideas for the lesson. These lessons are often more free-forming based on students' reactions, and they provide students with substantial time for discovery and investigation. So, for example, students might be provided more time on an activity if it appears that they would benefit from it; conversely, if the teacher-artist team believes it is time to move on to another activity, adjustments are made to the lesson.

When teaching lessons to the students, the artists often demonstrate and model techniques, coach students on artistic components, and provide general support and training to teachers. The teachers, on the other hand, introduce the lesson, establish classroom norms, and push forward the content objectives. Over time, the lines between artist and teacher become increasingly blurred as the teacher learns more about teaching through the arts and as the coach learns more about the students and the teaching process.

## Shifts in Affective and Cognitive Beliefs

Our research indicates that teachers observed shifts in students' beliefs about themselves as learners as a result of the artist-teacher relationship in the classroom. This was especially true of ELL students. Our results also suggest that teachers made important shifts in their own beliefs about their students. Given the connection to the arts, we might have expected to find that the teachers primarily observed shifts in students' affective beliefs. However, the results of our study suggest that teachers also made shifts in their beliefs about students' cognitive abilities (Bennett et al., 1999).

In the realm of affective beliefs, teachers recognized that teaching through the arts had an impact on students' self-confidence, on their motivation to participate in class, and on their self-esteem and sense of self-worth. Many teachers noted that their students responded more positively to learning when they were being taught through the arts. Self-confidence related to a willingness among students to take greater risks, leading to greater understandings because students no longer felt that they couldn't do the work because they didn't understand it. Teachers, not surprisingly, reported that they began to see their students in new ways. Shy students were taking more active roles in the classroom; previously unmotivated students were extremely engaged in learning through the arts; and students who were reticent were observed communicating their ideas in ways that were meaningful. This was particularly true for English language learners and students not as comfortable with communicating their understanding through the traditional means of written and oral language.

In addition to recognizing that teaching through the arts can impact students' affective beliefs, teachers also recognized how teaching through the arts can impact their views of students' cognitive abilities. Their experiences working with the artists seemed to help teachers see their "lower" students as academically more competent. We found that teachers were not the only ones who recognized the positive contributions the otherwise identified "lower" students could make in class.

In fact, we also found that students began to see each other in new ways, recognizing each others' talents. Teachers also began utilizing the arts to assess student understandings of content matter.

## Changes in Instructional Practices

As one might guess, teachers make significant changes in their instructional practices as a result of their work with artists. They have

- Learned to engage students mentally and physically in the learning process
- Learned to provide students with opportunities to explore, investigate, and discover
- Learned to create new ways for students to represent their ideas
- Created new ways to assess students' understanding of the content
- Learned to be less inhibited when teaching in the classroom

Individualized coaching for teachers by artists has been successful even under the most strained condition. Teacher transformation through interaction with the arts and artists can create important changes in their understanding of the role arts can play in education.

1. Teachers' notion or definition of who is an artist expands.
2. Teachers' understanding of the artistic process is broadened from viewing art as the acquisition of a set of techniques and skills to incorporating the role of experimenting as an important aspect of the artistic process.
3. Teachers relate and apply the artistic process to academic learning by comparing the importance of experimenting to understanding concepts.
4. Teachers develop personally in the area of arts appreciation both in their reflections and in an awareness of their students' knowledge of the arts.

Though in the majority of classrooms teachers, coaches, and researchers described the coaching relationships positively, what became increasingly evident was that in the few classrooms with clear tensions between the coach and the teacher, many important things were still happening. The six following categories could be found in *all* classrooms regardless of the quality of the teacher-coach relationship. Keep in mind, again, that all the classrooms have ELL learners.

- Teachers (and other students) see students in new ways.
- Teachers reach more students, and more students get to "shine."
- Students get excited about learning art or other content.
- Students are exposed to the arts.
- Students are motivated and involved in learning.
- Students (and often the teacher) are involved in some risk taking.

# Documenting and Describing the Role and Importance of Sustained Support for Coaches

The coaches meet as a group with the program director every week to discuss the program and their work in the classroom. The meetings focus on sharing stories of what is happening in the classrooms as well as on brainstorming activities to do in specific partnerships. In general, the meetings focus on arts integration, as well as working with challenging teachers.

Coaches' meetings provide security and support where trust and confidence are key and risk taking occurs. Camaraderie creates a sense of program ownership and reinforces a sense of flexibility, and modeling in terms of a process of brainstorming emanates back to teachers. The sustained nature of the meetings has created a history, complete with "case studies" of past experiences, that the coaches draw upon to inform new situations.

In addition to setting the stage for risk taking, certain philosophical tenets and practices emerge.

- Basic beliefs about art and arts in education are reinforced. "Art is really basic, and this is validated through the coaches meetings."
- Attention to what is possible drives the philosophy of the coaches. "Through this job I'm in contact with teachers and coaches and can see how that brings that much variety, different ways of doing things, and different processes. It has made me more of a believer in the creative process, more than I was already."
- A culture of invention is created, valued, and reinforced. "It is nice to know we don't have limitations; we didn't have a set way to go; we could just try it and see how it felt, and it was just real organic in the process and nothing was a mistake. I mean all of that made it real easy to try things and push yourself where you think you couldn't get pushed."
- Coaches are motivated to exhibit and/or perform. "[The coaches meetings] have inspired me to try new things, but also to do it more as an artist. I think it's gotten me kind of motivated to do more or branch out in different directions."

# Identifying and Describing the Factors That Support Sustained Change for Teachers

Overall, SUAVE is a successful and powerful model for professional development. Collaborating with artists and incorporating the artistic process into practice have challenged SUAVE teachers to risk trying new things in their classrooms. In doing so, teachers have felt that they and their students have benefited. For change to occur, Fullan (1999) underscored the importance of "keeping anxiety in balance, simultaneously provoking and containing it" (p. 61). The design of the SUAVE program has helped to both "provoke" and "contain" anxiety, thus promoting teacher learning. The tensions have provoked anxiety in both teachers and coaches. However, certain structural components of the SUAVE program have helped contain this anxiety and turn the tensions into learning opportunities. Specifically, SUAVE teachers have highlighted the following key structural components of the program: long-term involvement, support communities, customized classroom coaching, and the program philosophy of teaching through the arts. Other professional development programs might take notice of these structural components, since they have been successful in helping SUAVE teachers learn from tensions rather than simply be frustrated by them.

## Long-Term Involvement

SUAVE helps contain anxiety by allowing sufficient time for tensions to be addressed and resolved. Teachers are given two years to explore teaching and learning through the arts. Since teachers and coaches often arrive with differing goals and priorities, this extended period of time allows them to negotiate common understandings. Furthermore, a teacher and a coach are paired for an entire year. The long-term nature of this partnership provides an incentive for both to work though any serious differences so that the relationship can be both productive and enjoyable. Finally, the coaches are rotated yearly, so each teacher has the opportunity to work with two different coaches. This exposes the teacher to two artists, each with a different artistic specialty and personality, thus broadening the teacher's experiences with and understanding of the artistic world.

## Support Communities

Anxiety can also be contained by the support provided by others engaged in the same experiences. In SUAVE, both teachers and coaches are supported emotionally and intellectually throughout the coaching process. First, since ten teachers per school participate in SUAVE, each teacher has nine immediate colleagues with whom s/he can brainstorm ideas and share activities, fears, and excitement. Furthermore, teachers develop camaraderie with teachers from other schools as teachers from all SUAVE sites meet at the in-services. Second, all of the coaches are also supported. Each week, they meet as a group with the program director. During these meetings, they share artistic techniques and brainstorm ideas about potential lessons and ways to interact with teachers more effectively. In addition, the coaches provide an incredible support network for each other (more is written about these meetings in Chapter 10).

## Customized Classroom Coaching

The collaborations between the teaching and artistic worlds are most obvious in the classroom when new ideas are being explored. SUAVE's weekly coaching pushes teachers to try new things, but, as one fifth-grade teacher explained, "with a safety net," since the coach is actually present when the teacher is taking these risks. Thus, teachers are held accountable for trying to teach through the arts, but this accountability comes with substantial classroom support that helps to contain anxiety. In contrast, many professional development programs provide great ideas at in-services, but teachers are expected to implement these ideas without any follow-up support in their classrooms.

The customized nature of SUAVE's coaching further helps teachers in terms of taking risks. SUAVE coaches do not provide a canned program, but rather negotiate with each teacher to provide individualized assistance. Thus, a teacher can more easily see the relevance of teaching through the arts in his or her own classroom. Through this customized coaching, students in SUAVE classrooms experience some incredible lessons, and their unexpected excitement and learning often encourages teachers to continue trying new ideas.

### Program Philosophy of Teaching through the Arts

Given the pressures of an overstuffed curriculum, tensions should be expected whenever teachers are asked to add anything else to the list of things they are required to cover. However, SUAVE's basic approach of emphasizing teaching *through* the arts (rather than *about* the arts) is a clever hook for enticing teachers to work with the arts. Rather than suggesting additional content, SUAVE helps to contain anxiety by presenting the arts as a teaching methodology that can be used to teach the *existing* curriculum in a different, and potentially better, way. Interestingly, even though the program focuses on teaching core curriculum through the arts, teachers and students have also often become more interested in the arts themselves after seeing their power in other areas of the curriculum.

## Final Notes

At this point you're probably wondering whether you can integrate the arts without an artist or the structure of SUAVE to guide you. Simply put, yes. Of course, if you can bring artists into your classroom, all the better. If I had my wish, every school would have an artist-in-residence as well as visual art, music, theater, and dance teachers. Every teacher would integrate the arts into the classroom as an ordinary way of approaching the challenges of teaching in multicultural and multilingual settings. Without arts specialists, you can still integrate the arts. There are many ideas and lessons throughout the following chapters. Hopefully, they will be an initial step from which you'll want to jump. Once you take that leap, you will never stop.

## References

ASCD. (1998). *Arts education: A cornerstone of basic education.* Alexandria, VA: Association for Supervision and Curriculum Development Curriculum Update.

Ball, D. L., & Cohen, D. K. (1999). Developing practice, developing practitioners: Toward a practice-based theory of professional education. In L. Darling-Hammond & G. Sykes (Eds.), *Teaching as the learning profession* (pp. 3–32). San Francisco: Jossey-Bass.

Bennett, T. (2000). *Teacher change in professional development: Impacting teachers' culture through the arts.* Paper presented at the American Educational Research Association (AERA) Meeting, April, New Orleans, LA.

Bennett, T., Goldberg, M., Jacobs, V., & Wendling, L. (1999). *Teacher learning in professional development: The impact of an 'artist as mentor' relationship.* Paper presented at the American Educational Research Association (AERA) Meeting, April, Montreal, Canada.

Bennett, T., Jacobs, V., & Goldberg, M. (1999). *The power of multiple learning environments in professional development.* Paper presented at the American Educational Research Association (AERA) Meeting, April, Montreal, Canada.

Carson, R. (1956). *The sense of wonder.* New York: Harper and Row.

Fullan, M. G. (1999). *Change forces: The sequel.* Philadelphia, PA: Falmer Press.

Fullan, M. G., & Miles, M. B. (1992). Getting reform right: What works and what doesn't. *Phi Delta Kappan, 7* (10), 744–752.

Goldberg, M. (1997). *Arts and learning: An integrated approach to teaching and learning in multicultural and multilingual settings.* New York: Longman.

Goldberg, M. (1998). *Arts ain't fluff: Examining the impact of teacher/artist collaboration on children's academic achievement.* Address delivered to the Faculty Colloquia at California State University San Marcos, November 12.

Goldberg, M. (2000). *The mirrored selves (thanks Duke): Practicing professional development.* Paper presented at the annual conference of the American Educational Research Association, April, New Orleans, LA.

Goldberg, M. (2001). *Arts and learning: An integrated approach to teaching and learning in multicultural and multilingual settings,* 2nd ed., New York: Longman Publishers.

Goldberg, M., Bennett, T., & Jacobs, V. (1999). *Artists in the classroom: A role in the professional development of classroom teachers.* Paper presented at the American Educational Research Association (AERA) Meeting, April, Montreal, Canada.

Goldberg, M. R., & Bossenmeyer, M. (1998). Shifting the role of arts in education. *Principal, 77* (4), 56–58.

Jacobs, V. (2000). *What happens when the artistic world and a teacher's world meet?* Paper presented at the American Educational Research Association (AERA) Meeting, April, New Orleans, LA.

Jacobs, V., Goldberg, M., & Bennett, T. (1999). *Teaching core curriculum content through the arts.* Paper presented at the American Educational Research Association (AERA) Meeting, April, Montreal, Canada.

Jacobs, V., Goldberg, M., & Bennett, T. (2002). Uncovering artistic identity while learning to teach through the arts. In *Passion and Pedagogy.* New York: Peter Lang Publishers.

Little, J. W. (1990). The mentor phenomenon and the social organization of teaching. *Review of Research in Education, 16,* 297–351.

McClure, R. M. (1999). Unions, teacher development, and professionalism. In G. A. Griffin (Ed.), *The education of teachers: Ninety-eighth yearbook of the National Society for the Study of Education* (pp. 63–84). Chicago: University of Chicago Press.

Sparks, D., & Hirsh, S. (1997). *A new vision for staff development.* Alexandria, VA: Association for Supervision and Curriculum Development.

Thompson, C. L., & Zeuli, J. S. (1999). The frame and the tapestry: Standards-based reform and professional development. In L. Darling-Hammond & G. Sykes (Eds.), *Teaching as the learning profession* (pp. 341–375). San Francisco: Jossey-Bass.

# 3

# *Loving the Logistics: An Arts Administrator's Experience*

## Leah Goodwin

*Leah Goodwin with a puppet she created.*

### KEY CONCEPTS

- Partnerships
- The role of an arts center or institution in partnerships
- Collaboration
- Commitment
- Funding
- Building an infrastructure

For the past thirty years, there has been an ongoing debate about the tools, values, and attributes of arts education programs. There have been studies, statistics, and research, and all of them lead to one conclusion: the arts will provide opportunity for a child's educational excellence, personal development, and growth. To me, the core of the issue has been responsibility and funding. Is providing arts education school districts' responsibility? They are plagued with low test scores and budget cuts. They have an increasingly diverse student population. Are arts organizations responsible for ensuring that the visual and performing arts are introduced to and shared with youth? I have always believed that it is a shared responsibility. Because we know arts education works, all of us, artists and educators, should do the best we can to make it a presence in our schools.

In July 1994 I had the unique opportunity to work in a new multidisciplinary arts organization, the California Center for the Arts, Escondido. When I came on board there was an established education advisory committee, a separate education department, a plan, and a budget. The center opened in October 1994. After many years of supporting traditional artists in residency programs, SUAVE gave me the chance to take arts education support to the next level. More than a one-year plan where the art enters and the teacher leaves, SUAVE is unique because it works by building a partnership between artist (as coach) and educator.

In this decade, partnership is the name of the game when it comes to developing programs that provide good professional development and collaboration, ownership, and optimal success. The SUAVE program was created as a way to bring the arts back to the schools, to support educators, and to install a new methodology for teaching all subjects using the arts as a tool. The name SUAVE was given right at the beginning. Being a Spanish acronym, it was appropriate when looking at school districts with as much as 70 percent Latino enrollment at many sites.

Along with the partnership came mutual commitment and responsibility. In creating this program, it was decided that the California Center for the Arts should become the lead funding agency with financial responsibility. The center hired the artists and used the education director and staff time to implement the work. The other partners had strong financial commitments as well. California State University San Marcos (CSUSM) provided Dr. Goldberg with a distinguished teacher award, giving her release time to direct the program. Subsequently, the office of the vice president for academic affairs at CSUSM contributed (and continues to contribute) release time in the form of two course releases per year to Dr. Goldberg on an ongoing basis as part of the university budget. The school sites allocated funds for substitute teachers so that participating staff could attend five in-service training days, as well as providing supplies and curricular guidance. This arrangement allowed the art center to engage funders at the state and local levels as well as foundations that believe in supporting education but might not ordinarily give funds to an educational entity or school district.

At the center this commitment to the artists and education tied in with the educational philosophy and mission to create strong educational programs that support the statewide visual and performing arts (VAPA) framework. The education advisory committee was as a critical link in the success of the program. It is made up of presidents from the area state university and community college, superintendents from three school districts, principals, interested philanthropists, a representative from the County Office of Education, representatives from a few other local art agencies, and key educators who worked in arts or cultural affairs outreach positions in the area. This combination of resources and decision makers made it easy to get a resolution of support for arts education from all three participating school districts.

A critical point in the growth of SUAVE was when the California Arts Council (the statewide arts agency) opened new categories of funding for arts education, calling for a collaboration between a local art agency and a local education agency. As most agencies applied for planning grants, SUAVE had already finished its pilot year, and the center applied for expansion funding. The uniqueness of the program allowed SUAVE to receive the largest grant in the state, renewable for three years. This pivotal moment allowed the program to grow from three schools to six schools in Escondido. That same year, the Escondido Union School District, began to examine its visual and performing arts programs. In the curricular development meeting, educators decided to adopt SUAVE as the visual and performing arts program for kindergarten through fifth grade. With this adoption came a commitment from the school district to match the funds dollar for dollar. SUAVE was placed in eight schools in Escondido, with a plan to reach all twenty K–5 schools within three years. The same year, two low-achieving schools, one elementary school and one middle-school, allocated specific government funds to have bilingual SUAVE artists help build the curriculum for their underperforming and second language students. The program grew from serving three schools to serving twelve schools in year two, and the goal was to reach all Escondido schools by year five.

I remember being asked in an interview what my goal was for the program. I answered, "I would like SUAVE to be in every school in Escondido." As an administrator, I thought about sustainability. The brainchild of a few was growing and working. In the midst of the success, it was important to retain the intention of the partnership at all times. I found it useful to continue to support the team meetings. At a place where some people would let go of a program, I was compelled to give more—as much time as necessary to secure stability and growth. My involvement was most needed in working with the new levels of management staff, at school sites, and with the new artists.

The SUAVE program partnership affected a system funding change. In the next two years, the California Department of Education developed a grant to assist existing partnerships that had received California Arts Council funding to provide art-specific educational activities to schools. Of special note was the wording of the grant, which encouraged using substitute teacher time as a match, having an advisory committee, using arts integration as a tool for learning, and paying for transportation. This, as well as requests for presentations from the directors, made us realize that we were developing a model program.

At the center the SUAVE program became half of the educational department budget. A full-time program manager was needed to manage the schedules;

a full-time artist position with a benefits package was developed, and more artists were hired. The teacher in-service training days doubled, and monthly hands-on training for all teachers at "SUAVE Mondays" was implemented. To spread the word, an annual curriculum fair showcased the many projects that were created during the year, and curricular collections were distributed to educators who expressed interest in using the arts to support the curriculum. As of January 2000, SUAVE was operating in twenty schools with two thousand students. The center's staff included thirteen artists and one and a half full-time administrators. The program received more than $100,000 of government, corporate, and foundation funding in addition to the financial support of all its partners.

Integrating the SUAVE program and educator needs across the center's visual and performing arts programming was a part of the annual planning. Having access to a variety of world-class artists who provide entertainment to the public, to the schools, and to the center's museum created special opportunities. The performing arts department contracts around fifty presentations annually; the education department provided around thirty school performances annually. Special care was taken to look at the artists' offerings and talents when booking a show to see if there were opportunities for educational support and enhancements. Over the years artists such as Bella Lewistsky, Marcel Marceau, Andes Manta, Ballet Hispanico, and a variety of musicians, theater artists, puppeteers, and storytellers have provided special programs for teachers. This addition also gave a boost to regional artists. The museum exhibitions have also been a tool for learning and a source for education and creativity at all levels. Every SUAVE teacher visited the museum and created a visual arts curricular project at least twice a year.

The beauty of the SUAVE program also lies in its creativity and its ability to grow. With State Department of Education grants, we were able to take a successful eight-week visual arts curriculum developed by artist Kim Emerson, "Art Time Travel," and expand it for use in every fourth grade in the San Marcos, Escondido, and Valley Center School Districts. The curriculum serves as in-classroom training for educators. Each lesson has supplies, a transparency, and a project outline. There are ten baseline questions for the students and teacher at the beginning of the session, and the same ten questions are asked at the end to evaluate the educational value of the project. Initial funding supported the development of art and dance time travel; the next year music, theater, and photography time travel were created and implemented. Fourth- and fifth-grade classrooms were chosen as the target because there are specific benchmarks for the VAPA framework at these ages. These eight-week programs have been shared with thousands of students and educators. The next step is to consider publishing them and offering teacher training for implementing this tool.

As an outgrowth of the CSUSM partnership, eight artists, four educators, a CSUSM representative, and I were granted Fullbright-Hays scholarships to attend a three-week workshop on the role of puppetry in education sponsored by the Center for Cultural Resources in Udaipur, India. The idea was for artists and teachers to learn ways to use puppetry in education from experts. The trip also took the participants to cultural sites in India, such as the Taj Mahal, as well as to many

*Sudipta Dhruva, SUAVE liason in India, with Abel Silvas, SUAVE arts coach.*

schools where they not only learned about education in India, but also presented workshops for Indian teachers and students.

Recently I was asked to reflect on a profound moment in my professional and educational growth and development, and I immediately thought of that trip to India. At the Krishna Muti School in Sahadri, in the middle of the countryside, two hundred young people live with their teachers. Even though they miss their families in Bombay, they are happy to be at this school. These open-eyed, loving, and questioning youth are concerned about the environment, the air and the water, pollution and cars. They question life, wearing watches, and death; they discuss God and goodness. They learn by questioning, and they are encouraged to use all of their intelligence to do so. They sing, dance, and create ceramics and batik works in the art studio; they learn the basic educational curriculum in a format that suggests self-expression and nurtures creativity.

At the end of each day teachers, the principal, and students climb to the top of a hill in the Pune Valley, where they silently spend fifteen minutes watching the sunset. They reflect upon the day, releasing all the things that were not good and keeping all of the good things. Today, whenever I am watching a sunset or looking for a happy thought, I see their wise and questioning faces. Part of me wanted to stay there, to teach, to learn, to make a small difference in a big way. Maybe a part of me did stay. I know that I will never forget the experience, the belief in young people, the universal use of art as a tool for opening the mind of a child, and the love and passion of the educators we encountered on our journey.

The SUAVE program is a lesson in building the infrastructure with a belief in the good of the program and the flexibility to change to serve constituents. The program is always growing and always training, reaching out to more school districts and looking at serving older youth as well as supporting after-school programs. It has been a true joy to be a part of the partnership that created SUAVE. When people try to commend one partner—the college, or the center, or the district—for an excellent program, we stand together and say, yes, this is *our* grant-winning, award-winning arts education program.

So, if you find yourself embarking on a collaboration like this one, do it for a purpose. Even though the benefits, such as funding, rewards, prestigious grants, and the scholarship, were realized in our program, that was not the intent. The intent was and is to bring the arts back to education, to support educators, and to inspire the love of learning in young people. Be clear in partner responsibilities, develop a strong yet succinct mission, and enjoy yourself.

This program has been a highlight in my career and in my life; it has validated my belief in the arts as a tool for learning and has allowed me to create personal and professional friendships. Of course it was a lot of hard work, but each hour was balanced out with one "magical SUAVE moment" after another.

# 4

# *Principal as Advocate, Leader, and Supporter*

## Interview with Lydia Vogt

*Principal, Valley Center Primary School, and President, California Arts Educators Association.*

*Lydia Vogt, SUAVE principal.*

### KEY CONCEPTS:

- Administrator as arts advocate in ELL settings
- Advice to other administrators
- Keeping up to date with research
- Keeping up to date with local and national organizations
- Assessment, testing, and wonder
- Writing arts objectives into lesson plans
- Art-rich classroom environments
- Parent communications

*This chapter highlights the thoughts and ideas of Lydia Vogt, an elementary school principal who is also the president of the California Arts Educators Association. She was interviewed by Merryl Goldberg, editor of this book.*

I have always been involved in the arts. I come from a family of artists, and I have been surrounded by arts my whole life. When I was an elementary school teacher, art was an important part of my curriculum because I believed in it and enjoy doing art myself. It carried over as something important to me as a teacher to provide to the students. In the mid-1980s there was an invitation for a summer institution for professional development in the arts (it later became the California Arts Project), and I was selected by my principal to apply. That was the beginning of my involvement with what was to become the California Arts Project and many other things. Since then, probably the California Arts Project has been the main touchstone for a lot of the projects that I have done. I subsequently started attending the state conferences of the California Arts Education Association (CAEA). In the early 1990s I started working with the organization of the board on the southern area and then the CAEA state board. Recently, I was elected president of the California Arts Education Association. It's an honor and a large responsibility.

Being a principal in a small district and having a district that supports me in my arts focus has allowed me to have an effect beyond my own classroom. I think that one of the main reasons I went from being a classroom teacher to being an administrator was to touch more children. As a principal, I have six hundred children every year, and I can promote the arts at my site.

Valley Center–Pauma is a small district. As a result, I have the opportunity to influence the other administrators. Being the "art expert" in the district, I have been able to bring in-services, information, and activities related to the arts. Whereas in a big district you might get lost, in a small district I have been able to do whatever I can to keep arts in the schools. We have incredible teachers with individual interests and talents, many of whom have an understanding of the importance of art in classroom settings. We have two schools that have chosen the arts as their SIP focus (a three-year period when you are focusing on one curricular area in professional development). It has been a way of keeping the arts alive even during the most recent back-to-basics movement and the emphasis on standardized testing. We've been able to keep the arts going. I think a lot of that has come from the teachers themselves.

### What advice would you give to principals to keep or bring arts into the schools, especially in schools with a high second language learning population?

I think that administrators need to be informed. There are a lot of ways to do that. We're very busy people, and it's hard to find the time to keep up. My association with the California Arts Project, the CAEA, and the National Art Education Association (NAEA), has provided access to a lot of materials. The NAEA has files on everything from how to evaluate an arts program to how to set up an arts classroom. The National Music Association has similar information for evaluating music programs. I think because most administrators are probably not coming from an arts specialist background, it is very difficult, especially at the secondary level, to evaluate how a drama teacher is doing or how an art teacher is doing. You can certainly evaluate methodology and what's going on in organization, etc. But you need some sort of background, some sort of information system to know whether they are doing a good job within the content of that discipline.

Contact with professional organizations is also important. You don't have to be a member yourself, but look at what's going on, use the resources provided by those organizations, and have staff members who are member of those professional organizations act as resources, too. I think encouraging your teachers, especially the specialists, to become members of those organizations is extremely important so that they have that contact. The more rural your district is, the smaller it is, the more important it is to have those contacts because you tend to be very insular.

County offices can also provide support where you do not have a specialist in your district. There are also professional conferences that have administrative strands. I know that the California Art Education Association has a one-day strand in each conference for administrators. The focus this year was the new VAPA (visual and performing arts) standards that were adopted by the state board. Getting the administrators up to date on the standards is especially important. Just as we would never dream of not being knowledgeable about our language arts standards, it is important for an administrator to have a working familiarity with the visual and performing arts standards. We are sometimes under the impression that the arts are one area. But they are four areas, so it is a broad expectation of both teachers and administrators to be familiar with all that content. However, getting up to a knowledgeable level is really important in terms of what an administrator can do to support the arts.

Another way administrators can support an effective arts program is in allotting time. Time is important. Teachers need the opportunity to teach the arts without worrying that doing an art lesson is wrong. Recognizing that there are standards and that the arts are an important part of a well-rounded education is key. Then validate that by allowing teachers to have access to professional development that gives the skills to teach arts.

In California we don't have the luxury of having many arts specialists at the elementary level. There may be some music teachers. However, if you look at the statistics, there are very few art teachers in the public school system. Those at the elementary level are often funded through the teacher-parent club. Thus, it is usually the responsibility of the classroom teacher to introduce and teach arts. Unfortunately, most teachers without arts background do not feel comfortable doing that, so it is up to administrators to emphasize the importance of the arts as a part of every child's basic education. Teachers need access to tools and materials such as instruments, textbooks, and visual arts materials. Materials for visual arts lessons need not be expensive or have a huge impact on budget. Bring in professionals to do some in-service. Fund teachers to participate in state projects like the California Arts Projects and the Summer Institute, and send them to conferences so they can gain a basic level of skill in an arts discipline.

*Lydia Vogt, SUAVE principal.*

It is also important to recognize that if we're not requiring teachers to show that they have some sort of curriculum in the arts, we're sending the message that the arts are not important. At this point our standardized testing does not include any questions on the arts; that content knowledge is not being testing and therefore at some levels is not being valued. It then falls back on the administrator to say that the arts are important.

There are a number of ways I think we can support teachers in this realm. In relation to the assessment, we need to help teachers find ways of looking at children's learning in and through the arts. That doesn't mean that you have to give them a grade on the product that they have made. It does mean that you need to evaluate what your instruction has been and what the students have learned, so that you know if you have been successful in teaching it. That may involve some sort of product assessment, or it may not. For instance, if you look at standard 4, Aesthetic Valuing, in the California Frameworks for Visual and Performing Arts, students should be able to look at their own work as well as the work of others and make an informed judgment about it. If they can do that, we know they have the vocabulary and the knowledge they need. A written test is not necessary. I also ask teachers to write an objective in the arts every year. They are becoming familiar with the standards, and they are taking the time to not only teach that objective but also assess how well students did. It is another way to make focus on the arts part of the basic curriculum.

**Can you give me an example of what an objective would be?**

The last couple of years, our first-grade classes have had a visual arts objective that works with a standard in artistic perception that says that children should be able to use an arts vocabulary to show their knowledge of visual arts. Because it stresses vocabulary, it transfers to writing very nicely. As their assessment of whether the children had learned this vocabulary, teachers had children write about the artwork they had done. They wrote in a subjective way about feeling and expressive content, but they also wrote about their use of color, textures, and other elements. Their writing reflected the vocabulary they had learned that year. The teachers were then able to evaluate whether the students had learned the vocabulary and could apply it to pictures they had done themselves.

**The kids do this in both English and Spanish?**

They do. In the bilingual classrooms, the children wrote in Spanish. Teachers translated the vocabulary for visual arts. In the two-way bilingual classes where children are learning in both languages, they can chose to write in Spanish or English. Visual arts are a wonderful place to do ELD (English Language Development). We have three ways to work with second language learners in Valley Center. We have our two-way program where they are learning in their first language while the second language is developed at the same time. We also have transitional classes, which are sheltered English classes that also provide first language support. We have clusters of English learners in those classrooms; they are basically English language classes. And then we have individual students who enter later in the year and are placed wherever we have room. They are basically in an English immersion program, but we give them support with pull-out or in-class help in their first language and for ESL.

In some cases in the transitional and the two-way program we used art reproductions to help develop vocabulary as ESL. Through looking at art reproductions and talking about them, students learned to use the vocabulary of the elements of art, texture, line, shape, and colors. It was a great way to develop some very specific vocabulary in English.

**Why do you think that, for ESL kids, the art is captivating, that it works?**

What we found is by choosing artwork that is representational, that actually contains a story, students are easily motivated. For instance, Thomas Hart Benton's painting, *The Wreck of Old 97*, is a painting of a train and a wagon that are about to collide. The horse is rearing, and the people are falling out of wagon; it's very exciting. It is Benton's commentary on the collision of modern life with old life, the industrialization of America. It's a wonderful painting, and it contains a great story. Where were these people going? Why don't the children have shoes on? The cornfield is almost surrealistic—as if the stalks of corn are trying to get away from the train. Is the wagon going to stop in time, and why is the train almost off the track? It contains a huge story. That kind of picture captivates the kids very quickly, and there's no language barrier to it. So as children begin to talk about it, it really encourages them to process what is happening regardless of what their first language is.

When the students start talking, if it's an ESL lesson, obviously their vocabulary and their past experience is going to limit what they are able to say in English. But what's going on in their minds is not limited. When you are using a story with words, not only is their ability to speak limited by their vocabulary and knowledge of English, but their ability to read what happened and process it is limited. You get into idioms, and it is difficult for students to imagine a story beyond their limiting reading vocabulary. With the picture, there is no limit, other than their own past experience and the image they are seeing. So they may not be able to express everything they are seeing, but they have the story in their minds just as much as a child in Chinese or English or any other language. So we found that using art reproductions is very successful in stimulating language.

Many of our students enter school with limited fluency in any language. This may be due to an impoverished background, cultural differences, prenatal substance abuse, or unknown factors. But what we do know is that if those children don't have a strong first language, it very difficult for them to learn a second language. That's why we have our two-way program. But we found that with the kindergarten and first-grade level, we need to do a lot of oral language development in their first language before beginning second language development. If they don't have a word for *winding* in their first language, teaching it to them in their second language makes very little sense.

**What's your sense with your classrooms here, because most of them are art rich, just describe a typical classroom. What does it look like? What does it feel like?**

I think because we are a primary school, kindergarten through second grade, the teachers are aware that a stimulating visual environment is important. In fact, if I have to do anything it's to ask them to tone it down because it's so enriching in the visual stimulation, especially for children who have any kind of attention deficit. So what you see is an environment that is rich with both print and the children's work displayed. I think that typically in any classroom you would find some form of artwork displayed. There are a number of teachers who have an artist of the month, so you might find pictures that were modeled after the type of work that some particular artist has done.

Music is important to us, too, although I think I could say that teachers don't feel as confident in that area, and if we were to have a specialist they would choose to have a music specialist. We see a connection between students' ability to keep a steady beat and their success in reading. We have done a number of in-services that had teachers beginning to feel comfortable about doing some type of rhythmic activities. They sing daily, and we put on several evening performances. The district has had both art and music textbooks since the mid-1980s, and as we grow it has been very good about providing funds so that teachers have those materials.

*Lydia, drawing from nature while studying in Veracruz, Mexico.*

Another support that an administrator needs to provide is encouragement and access. We have a number of first-grade teachers who participate in an arts rotation. One day a week three or four of them team up. One will be the drama person and will do some sort of theater activities. Somebody else is doing visual arts; somebody else is doing music. There maybe some movement, maybe a physical education component in there. It varies, but it gives the children access. Since we have the standards now, both the state standards and our own district standards, all teachers have a more specific curriculum on which to base what they are doing. They've had textbooks and have used those in the past. But having the standards will assist them. Theater rotations take two weeks to complete, so the teacher is able to use the same lesson for two weeks in a row. The groups include the bilingual classes in those rotations, so that the children are mixed with the education classes. They have access to different groups of friends, which is kind of nice too. You also might see plays going on. Those things really help make the curriculum more meaningful. They take whatever it is that they are reading and do some type of dramatization.

The teachers who have been here over a period of time have really gained a lot of knowledge from the SUAVE program. This year, having two different arts coaches on campus, we really have richness on campus that we haven't had before. The teachers are just thrilled with the schedule.

**Do you have any teachers who balk at this, or have to be convinced to teach through the arts, or have you set up a situation where it's so supported that people don't even question it?**

I think people here don't question it. In my interviews with teachers, when I first hire them, I talk about the importance of the arts. I give everyone that little poster, "How to Be an Arts Teacher." I think that if your expectations are that teachers will be doing lessons based on the standards, the arts are there. If the expectation that children will have the right to a good arts education is there, you don't have to be an arts person to do that. I guess there are teachers who need encouragement because they don't feel qualified, not because they don't believe in it. I truly believe that. I think that a teacher who has the kind of personality and the kind of belief system to want to become an elementary teacher believes the arts play a part in developing a whole person.

The hard part is the time issue. I would be kidding myself or you to say that time does not play a part. There's no way we have a perfect arts program here. We have a lot of arts here; we have the feeling of appreciating the arts here. But when you have standards in all of the areas that are so strongly tested in the upper levels, we can't ignore that. And we work constantly. That why it's so exciting to have Donna (a SUAVE coach) working with the kinesthetic learning module this year, because hopefully this will give teachers a way of doing some of those standards and true arts lessons and of seeing that they can not only accomplish the same thing but do it better.

**Have you ever had parents question arts in the classroom?**

You know I really can't say that I have. I certainly have had parents who will request a certain teacher because of the arts. I have had a parent or two who were concerned about too many arts activities. I spent just a little bit of time justifying and talking about the application of what the children were learning through arts activities. At the same time, I told the teacher that it was important for us to make sure that parents understand that this is not a frill—that there is a basic core of knowledge that students are expected to learn, just as within any other content area, and that how the teacher presents the information to the parent about what is happening in the classroom is crucial. In our weekly newsletters to parents, teachers have to write more than "we did a nice picture of flowers." They have to talk about what the students were learning.

I think what administrators can do is help teachers and parents understand. It's public relations. We need to be sure that when we talk about the arts, we don't present them as frivolous. You are always going to have people who aren't satisfied with one thing or another.

**What advice would you give administrators who may be on the fence?**

If you look at the school districts that have high test scores, obviously the student population is what is affecting those test scores. I don't think that there are better teachers or better curricula in those districts. But frequently those schools have an arts program. They have music teachers; they have an arts specialist. If you look at schools with high test scores in an area that has high-income parents, they find ways to provide the arts. Those parents want the arts in their programs. I think you could make the assumption that the arts are not hurting the test scores. That goes a long way. There is also growing evidence that there maybe some connection between some areas of the arts and student learning. We know that kids who participate in the arts throughout their elementary years do score higher on their college entrance exams.

It behooves us to be educated on what the arts can do, to be able to speak intelligently about why the arts are important. You need to be up on the most current early literacy research if you are an elementary school principal. Be aware of current arts research, too. And then think about how involved we all are in the arts. Whether we are opera buffs or listen to rap music or take photographs on vacations, it is hard to image the world without the arts. So if we recognize that it's important to us, why would we not allow that for our children? Understanding the importance of a strong, sequential, standards-based arts program for our kids, and then finding the way to help teachers teach that program, is where we have to go.

**When kids are working through the arts, how do you assess wonder, assuming that one believes that wonder is a key element in learning?**

Sure, there is curiosity to learn. I think that is such a fascinating idea. When I was in Washington this last summer, reading for the federal model arts program grants in the evaluation component, several applicants proposed investigating this idea. What I look for in the classroom is someone who is working with the teacher to improve his or her methodology to be a better teacher.

There are two things that are extremely important to me within the realm of the arts. One is the arts have a core content, a specific body of knowledge that is within the disciplines of the arts. This knowledge is as important as any other specific knowledge a student is supposed to learn. This is outside of the wonder and the joy and all the reasons we participate in the arts as human beings. In order for us to be true consumers of the arts, knowledge of this content is essential. The other area I believe in is that if something is important enough to teach, then it's important for us to try to assess what the children have learned. Given the time constraints we have these days, to assume that we would teach something and not somehow or another find out whether the kids have learned it makes absolutely no sense to me. I want to know about the wonder. I want to know about the joy. But I want to know if the children have learned warm and cool colors, if that's what I taught them. Somehow I have to find out if they learned it. In that viewpoint, assessment has to include some sort of evaluation by me as teacher. It may be purely teacher observation—that may be all that is needed. But still I would love to know what else we engender when we give students quality experiences in the arts.

**Maybe the wonder is the second part of that. To me, it seems like if a kid has learned warm and cool colors and then doesn't do anything with it, or doesn't do anything with it past that point of learning . . .**

You are absolutely right. I think what we are talking about is the artistic perception component of the framework or standards where that content is. But if you don't go into the creative expression, if you don't ever use that "beyond" to get the joy that comes from creating and experiencing, then what was the point of learning the content? So you have to have both. What I think you are talking about comes from the creative part—that's where the joy comes. That is the premise of the standards and the framework, and of everything we are doing when we say that the arts have to have meaning as art. It's wonderful to integrate. It's wonderful to see what they can do. But we have to value them as a curricular area themselves. Then when you do that creation, you have that joy and inspiration because you have the knowledge to do it. If you took a kid who has never had any experience with a particular art form, the level of joy and wonder that the child is going to experience is going to be much enriched, along with the knowledge of warm and cool colors. Do you see what I'm saying? I think there needs to be both.

We are learning more. How does a child learn to read? Why can one child read and another not? I think as we learn how the brain works, we will learn more and more about doing something in a creative sense, and how it impacts a very linear kind of reading or math activity. I suspect there is evidence that we will gain, but we're not there now, and there are so many other reasons to do the arts. So while that information might be very important, we should not tie it to whether or not to include the arts. We should include the arts, period.

# 5

# *The Many Languages of Art*

## Eduardo García
*SUAVE Coach (Guitarist)*

*Eduardo Garcia,
SUAVE arts coach.*

### *KEY CONCEPTS*

- Working as a bilingual artist in ELL settings
- Departures and destinations
- Teacher-artist partnerships
- Math and movement
- Singing
- Keeping alive several cultures in the classroom
- Special needs students

Working as a bilingual artist with teachers and students in north San Diego county has afforded me many opportunities for reflection on the role of the arts in building bridges between various ways of knowing. I think of these ways of knowing as departures and destinations, because people's ways of knowing are also organized by where they come from and where they are going. How we move through these departures and destinations is also varied and multidirectional, making each learning moment immensely rich with possibility. Here, where I am writing, we face challenges of bridging departures and destinations such as Spanish and English, poor and wealthy, white and nonwhite. We also have to build bridges between a diversity of learning styles (kinesthetic, verbal, aural, visual, tactile, and others) and that privileged form of learning and assessing on paper that dominates schools today.

In bridging departures and destinations, we encounter connections and commonalities that bring about a consciousness that different fields have many similarities and thus are closer to each other than we think; that children represent a wealth of styles and aptitudes, all of which are needed in our world and vital for the integral development of the child. The arts allow us to see those connections, showing us the diversity of interacting ways of knowing. Teaching through the arts empowers the teacher, the student, and the artist to meet in a neutral zone where no one is an expert and everyone turns into a learner.

The artist-teacher dynamic—at least in my experience—is a process with two basic parts. First, the two experts (the teacher in the arts of educating, and the artist in art techniques) exchange ideas on how to teach different areas of the curriculum. The model is conceived as a partnership, so the two experts use each other's knowledge to teach through the arts. After some time, they reach a curriculum area that neither has integrated through the arts. At this point, neither can lead or offer expert advice. Rather, this is the time to brainstorm and look for ways to integrate the arts into the curriculum. In other words, first artist and teacher dance the dance of using up their proven techniques, and then they move to that neutral zone where the students await them.

My objective, thus, as an artist is to open up the bridges connecting the places of departure and arrival so that these different languages, learning styles, and intelligences feel comfortable in the classroom and learning becomes dynamic and charged with excitement, passion, and joy. What I would like to do here is to illustrate, through a series of stories, how this all happens.

## Math and Movement

The relation of movement or music and mathematics is not hard to see. After all, music and dancing, like math, involve patterns. The challenge is teaching math, which is usually taught through paper and pencil and sitting at the desk, in a way that involves the student in movement. As a musician, this seemed obvious to me so I tried it. I used this activity to review, practice, and memorize tables of multiplication with students who already knew how to multiply.

The activity starts with skip counting. We do this by playing a version of the game "Twister." The circles on the floor are given different values—say they're worth two—and we ask a team of students to find the total if they cover eight circles. They have to count by two. After they learn this, we move to synthesize it into eight times two. At this point I introduce sound, movement, and the idea of rhythm. For this I group sounds in threes and choose a pattern according to the multiplication problems at hand. **Clap** clap clap times (crossing my arms) **clap** clap clap equals (positioning my arms in parallel planes) **clap** clap clap **clap** clap clap **clap** clap clap. Next I show them another level: **clap** clap clap **clap** clap clap X **clap** clap clap **clap** clap clap = **stomp** stomp stomp, **clap** clap clap **clap** clap clap (clap = 1, stomp = 10). Students like this and are excited to try it on their own. We then introduce the next level: **stomp** clap clap X **stomp** clap clap = spin, **stomp** stomp stomp **stomp, clap** clap clap **clap.** Here spin = 100.

Needless to say, students become excited and review every single multiplication problem they can think of and even go beyond; they create their own problems and perform them in front of the class going into the thousands and tens of thousands. In this way they create their own choreography while studying multiplication and creating a different language to express numbers and rhythm. The first thing I noticed after doing this activity was that this way of teaching and learning multiplication benefits kinesthetic learners who can not sit for long periods of time. But it also benefits paper learners who have never imagined that multiplication could be so dynamic. Finally, in a classroom of ELL students, this activity allows everybody to engage in the lesson regardless of language. Thus, students learn multiplication, and their learning is assessed without being hindered by students' limited English.

# Singing

Singing is a great way to invite people into a new language. In singing, everyone acquires words, phrases and concepts of the song. With this idea in mind, the first-grade bilingual class of Mrs. Z embarked on a lesson about sea life. The kids read and learned about the kinds of animals and plants that live in the sea. I introduced the Beatles' song "Yellow Submarine." They learned the melody. I asked them to change the words to suit our needs; they were to show me what they knew about sea life. I modeled the first line and guided them to write the new words together. Every time a child contributed an idea, we would sing it together to hear if it fit in the melody. Pretty soon they got the idea; they started to count syllables and fit the words to the melody. We thought of hand movements to go with the singing, rehearsed it several times, and presented in class. The students were very proud of themselves and of their "new" song. Here are some of the words:

*Octopus and jellyfish*
*shells and sharks, whales and squids*
*Hammerheads, electric eels*

*Seahorses and schools of fish*
*Coral reefs and seaweed*
*Live together not so deep*
*So we see so many crabs*
*Let's all of us dive so deep*
*We all live in a Yellow Submarine . . .*

Singing is also a way to question the concept of limited English and to discover the English language talents of all students. Sometimes, classrooms are not even equipped to make such discoveries, as was the case in Mr. D's classroom. When I arrived to teach a music lesson as part of a music time travel (a five-week series to teach fourth graders basic literacy in music), I discovered that there was not a working CD player in the room—it obviously was not an arts-rich environment. However, when I guided the class in composing lyrics about whales to a melody I provided them with, two girls, who up to that point hadn't said a word because of their purportedly limited English, contributed twenty lines following the seven syllables per line formula the melody required. We then proceeded to croon to a "Whale of a Song":

*Whales are the biggest mammals*
*Whales do migrate in winter*
*Whales have babies like people*
*Whales breathe through their spiracle*

Some fifth-grade (ELL) students were studying desert environments with their resource teacher, and to help them assimilate the information we sang the facts, which they themselves fit to the melody "I've Been Working on the Railroad." They included terms such as *arid, desert, dunes, snakes, lizards,* and *reptiles.* Third graders enjoyed putting together their own version of George Harrison's "Here Comes the Sun" to learn a food chain: sun feeds plankton plants feed tiny animals feed small-size fish feed middle-size fish feed the bigger-size fish. Second graders worked on bringing the book *Swimmy* to life. They made big colored fish, seaweed, and the other creatures in the story. After that, they put the words Swimmy pronounces—as he organizes the other fish to scare the big fish—to the music of the Beatles' "Come Together."

As these examples show, music, and the arts in general, can help students in language acquisition. From personal experience, I know this works. I grew up in the city of Juárez, across the border from El Paso, Texas. Nobody spoke English in my home as I was growing up. But my older brothers listened to radio stations from the other side of the border. We also watched television without really understanding the words. The number of hours I heard English probably did not exceed five or six a week. Nevertheless, this was of immense help in my own language acquisition, for it allowed me to acquire the phonetic aspect of the language before I ever studied grammar and syntax. By the time I learned English in college, I had a good part of the work done already, and that made matters easier.

Inhabiting two languages at once is comparable to living in a metaphor. Metaphor is the technique used by poets to take us on a journey through two worlds. The poet might say "Life is a dream, and dreaming is life," birth and death are the beginning and the end of that dream. If we then say life = dream and further say more explicitly that life is A and dream is B, it follows that A = B. Now, of course, we know, because common sense dictates that life is not a dream, that A ≠ B. In this way, the metaphor seems to both negate and equate two things, ideas, or objects at the same time. "Spanish is English" is a metaphor for dwelling in two languages even though we know it isn't so. People who speak both English and Spanish and mix them in a natural way live by this metaphor. Some writers have argued that "Spanglish," as the practice of mixing the two is known, signals the creation of a new language and that attempting to stop such a process is unrealistic and even undesirable. This kind of mixing of two usually separate realms can and, from the point of view of creativity, should be thought of as positive. Inhabiting two processes or intelligences is a metaphor, and metaphor is the natural condition for creativity.

## Keeping Several Cultures Alive in the Classroom

Mary Ellen O'Malley takes a picture of our ten-member puppetry group (two from the United States, two from the Indian state of Kerala, two from Sikkim, and the others from Andhra Pradesh, Uttar Pradesh, Maharashtra, Karnataka). We have just finished performing a puppet play I wrote. In it, Guitar, Drum, and Maracas attempt to form a friendship but are unable to. First, Guitar appears, making its sounds and looking for friends, and encounters Drum. As they cross paths, they attempt to communicate but are unable to. In frustration and bewilderment, they go their separate ways. Afterwards, Maracas appears, producing a hypnotic rhythm in search of friendship; it runs into Drum and Guitar, but no luck, no communication. They make other attempts at conversing, but each instrument tells the others to make sounds like it's making. The result is cacophony because they all keep producing their sounds but are not harmonizing or introducing any rhythm. Later, a child appears, whistling and singing. The child encounters the instruments one by one, and they say they have tried to make friends with the others but have failed. The child then teaches them that they have a common language. "Although you have different voices and sounds when combined in the right way they make up what is called music" says the little child. Thus, they learn a song together: "together, together, we can sing together." In this way, a hopeless situation turns into connection—communication is basic for understanding. That is the basic premise of this play. However, there are other ramifications as well.

In 1999 a group of fifteen artists, teachers, and arts administrators went to India on a Fullbright-Hays grant to study the role of puppetry in education. There were more than a hundred participants in the workshop. For a final project, we had

*Puppets used in storytelling originated in Rajastan, India.*

to present a puppet play. The first step was for each person to write a sketch for a play and turn it in for comments and critiques. Then each of the ten groups into which the participants were divided had to choose one sketch, develop it, make the puppets, practice the play, and present it. In the end, only two plays were chosen to be performed at the closing ceremony at which the director of the national center and other personalities from Delhi awarded certificates of completion. To my surprise, my play was chosen.

When we first turned in our plays (about a hundred of them), mine came back with the comment "ready to manipulate." The Indian teachers, seeing that mine had such a complimentary reaction from the staff running the workshop, immediately chose it for production. I was surprised because I had thought of my play as dealing with issues of difference in the United States and didn't yet realize what was to come.

The import of the play soon became obvious. As we started rehearsing, I suggested that the child puppet should speak in Hindi. According to experts, India has sixty-five live languages (Mexico has sixty-two; China has fifty-four; and five thousand are spoken in the world). The little Tower of Babel created by the child puppet character was a lesson in richness of culture, the problems of nation-building, and the danger of language and cultural erasure. Communication, I presumed, would be hard because of language differences. My decision to use the official language along with English touched upon the problem of erasing other languages in unifying of peoples and territory and privileging one language over others spoken by millions. However, the group worked exceptionally well. The production of the play allowed everyone to work on either producing puppets or manipulating them and memorizing lines. Thus, language differences were overcome by engaging the members of different cultures and languages in a common art project.

Out of the ten teachers in my group, only one was a monolingual speaker of Hindi, the official language of India. The two Kerala teachers spoke Malayalam and a little English. The others spoke an array of different languages (Kannada, Maharati, Telugu, Nepalese) but no English or Hindi. The exception was T.T. (from Sikkim), who spoke Bujan, Nepalese, Tibetan, a little English, and Hindi (his state became part of India in 1975). He communicated with his fellow Sikkim teacher in Nepalese. T.T. struggled for two days to translate a few lines I wrote for the child puppet. Finally, after a lot of preparation, we were more-or-less ready.

Notice that our play had been chosen for performance came at the last minute, and as the speakers made their speeches we feverishly rebuilt some of the puppets that were damaged during rehearsals and changed others following last-minute recommendations from the director about how to make them look better or bigger. The play went well, and the audience applauded. We were done. Our play showed music as a way to bridge different languages and puppetry as an art form that makes learning in a multilingual and multicultural setting possible.

We also face language issues here in southern California, and the role of the artist can become doubly important. Mr. H is out of ideas to teach English to his fifth graders. These are all second language learners. These students are recent arrivals, mostly from Mexico and Central America. They know how to read and write in Spanish, but they're just starting to learn English, and they pronounce the English words as if they were Spanish ones. So, Mr. H wants them to associate the sounds of English with how the words look. For this, he needs them to repeat the words over and over while looking at them. It has taken a lot of energy out him already. After brainstorming, the idea of a carnival arises. We design a phonemic exercise using music. More specifically, we use drumming and the idea of call and response used in African-based music of Latin America. The students are familiar with this musical feature because of the popularity of dance rhythms such as cumbia, son, mambo, and bossa nova.

Students wear flash cards of English syllables. We sit in a circle. Mr. H and I drum; he calls the first syllable of the word *operation* "o"; the group responds "o." This is repeated over and over, as the students read each other's flash cards until they figure out who has that syllable. That person dances her way through the aisle to the center of the circle and takes her place in the middle. "Per," calls Mr. H. "Per" responds the group, and the call and response is repeated over and over. The person wearing "per" dances to the center of the circle and takes her place alongside "o." Now we have "oper." Everybody chants the syllables as they are called forward. "A" calls Mr. H, and "a" responds the class. "A, a, a, a". A student stands up, dances to the center, and takes his place, and now we read "opera." "Tion, tion, tion, tion." Another student stands up and dances—she is not too shy to move in undulating motions—to the center. We finally have the complete word: *o-per-a-tion*. "Operation," Mr. H chants, and everybody responds. As we keep chanting the word, the students dance back to their places.

This process is repeated with other words from the same family: *cooperation, foundation, interrogation, assimilation, restoration, administration, recommendation.* After one family of words is danced and chanted this way, we chant and dance another family of words. The more we use this process, the more the students get comfortable with the idea of dancing and chanting. In fact, they start inventing their own steps as they chant and respond to the syllables being called. They also come up with other words they think are from the same family of words. This is no small feat, given that students of this age are acutely aware of their bodies and feel extremely awkward; the mere act of standing in front of the class requires a lot of courage. What could have been a very tedious process of repetition in order to learn new sounds has become a form of expression through dance and chanting and an affirmation of their cultural heritage. This last point is important to note.

In the process of assimilation, people run the risk of losing their culture of origin in exchange for the new culture in which they live. This exchange may or may not be acknowledged as it happens, but it is felt. If, instead of losing, the students gain, then assimilation need not be an erasure of identity, but rather the creation of a new one with elements of both cultures—and even many other cultures encountered in the new environment. With this activity, students add English to what they bring with them from their previous environment. This process of cultural exchange enriches, rather than impoverishes, them. As they participate in, and gain control of, the process of English language acquisition, they are actively involved and empowered as creators of new knowledge, identity, and culture—new paradigms of their cultural wealth.

When the English-only proposition was being debated and after it was approved by the California voters, teachers used me as a sounding board either to express discontent about the proposition or simply to ask for ways in which to bridge the gap until appropriate materials were developed for ESL students. In these instances, the use of arts eased the pressure on both the teacher and the students to produce immediate results. Teachers were happy to be able to promote a caring atmosphere of learning (any learning!) under immense pressure. Other times, my presence in the classroom seems to ease an otherwise rigid situation where the boundaries between languages appear hopelessly insurmountable and even adversarial.

Recently, a teacher in a predominantly white, middle- and upper-middle-class school replied to my noting the level of achievement on the part of students, "They have the genetic and material advantage." At the same time, this teacher expressed anti-bilingual education sentiments and views. Obviously, this teacher's perspective is not shared by most teachers, but even in this context my arts activities rub against the grain of such unquestioned views. Kids find music and arts from different parts of the world to be interesting and exciting. The arts give them opportunities to show aspects of themselves that are normally hidden in the classroom. The bully writes a sensitive poem; the student with limited English contributes many lines of lyrics to a song; the jock enjoys weaving. The arts also allow students to appreciate cultural practices from other countries.

As an arts coach, I witness students expressing and using abilities through the arts that are normally ignored because we don't devise ways of noting such abilities and we may end up thinking of them as unimportant. We notice only what we have words to describe. The arts provide us with many opportunities to observe such abilities in action. These are the moments we as artists and teachers should capture and describe in order to better understand them.

## Different Intelligences

I didn't seem to be getting through to Mrs. J's class; they didn't seem to remember anything from one lesson to the next. I wondered aloud, "Am I going too fast? Am I doing something wrong?" The teacher reassured me that I was doing fine; "they never get any of this, keep going." "What is the problem, then?" "This is a class with special needs." I learned, then, that there were students with little English, ADD, and disabilities, all in the same class. Sometimes a school will put all these students in one class. Mrs. J's was one of them. At the same time, I was teaching the same material to a GATE (gifted and talented) class, and they seemed to have no trouble at all with it. I visited both classes twice a week for five weeks to teach music time travel. The surprise came at the end, when it became clear that each class had learned something different from the series. The class with special needs had discovered, through music, a way to make sense of complex cognitive processes.

In the five weeks we studied concepts that have driven the development of music: humans imitating the sounds of nature, monophony, polyphony, rhythms from around the world, homophony, and some aspects of twentieth-century music. In this last unit we talk about the effect of the two world wars on the artists and composers of the first half of the century and explain why many of them moved into atonal, dissonant music. We then hear some examples of musicians who have looked for inspiration in sounds and imagery from the environment: cities, nature. In the end, we are ready to explore our own world of music and create what I call a sound sculpture.

For this, we take a theme familiar to both classes: the water cycle. Students tell me the stages in the cycle: accumulation, evaporation, condensation, and precipitation. I direct them to imagine the sounds these stages might produce. They all know the sound of rain (precipitation), but the other stages are open for exploration. So, they help in discovering sounds in our own environment of the classroom that can convey those stages in the water cycle. After a while we find them. They are all very soft: shaking a piece of paper sounds like precipitation; accumulation sounds like pencils rolled between the hands; evaporation is matched by rubbing the walls with bare hands; condensation approximated by thumbing the pages of books. Everybody participates joyfully in the experience.

Conducting a four-beat pattern, I treat the experience as a regular piece of music (which it is not) and signal them to change actions according to the number we had previously assigned each of the stages of the water cycle. Students in the GATE class, who find the facts and sequences of the water cycle easy to grasp, are not interested in this activity. Not so the students in the class with special needs. Their faces light up with pleasure. They sense they have created something magical! We repeat the piece over and over. They're fascinated. We tape it and listen to it attentively. They have understood the purpose of the activity. They are extremely stimulated by it. Why?

After I finished with those classes, I continued trying to find an answer to why the two classes reacted so differently to the last activity in the series. In place of an answer, I offer my response to what happened and how I related to it.

First, the image that came to my mind is that of someone who all of a sudden discovers what the world looks like when you hold a fishing net and look through it. You suddenly see the world chopped up in discrete chunks that can be easier to understand. The "needy" class experienced a Cartesian vista of the world. They don't know they experienced that; they don't have the verbal tools to say so; but is that what happened? Maybe. But this was not a vista or view of the world in Cartesian terms because it wasn't visual; it was an aural experience, and it definitely affected them. I think I know just how.

As a musician I know that performing music allows me to widen my self-extension in the world in the sense that I have to use my hearing on two levels. One is central hearing; this helps me concentrate on the part for which I am responsible. The other one is peripheral in nature; this helps me be aware of what other musicians are playing—it helps me listen to everybody's part. Thus, my perception of myself extends to include the other musicians. We make the whole musical performance together; we act as one entity. My sense of myself extends to the whole group without erasing my individuality. This knowledge is uniquely experienced in performing music because it takes place in real time and makes use of both central and peripheral hearing. One does not have time to think about it, so to speak. Since a Cartesian perception of the world uses linear thinking, it takes time to conceptualize. One learns about the world by dividing it and studying its individual features; in this way we slow down a particular process to better understand it. In Mrs. J's class, however, through music, we sped up this process with surprising results. Mrs. J's students showed me they were capable of something the other class wasn't able or didn't want to achieve. This activity enabled them to integrate pairs of opposites: the regular and the irregular, the formless and the formal, the timeless and the timed, that which is outside time and that which is chronometric.

The capacity to integrate pairs of opposites is a creative act. In *The Act of Creation* (1964), Arthur Koestler describes the act of creation through the "logic of laughter," which he defines as "the perceiving of a situation or idea in two self-consistent but habitually incomparable frames of reference." These students were able to conceptualize and grasp, through music, abstract cognitive relations seldom identified in the elementary classroom. By using their hearing on the two levels I described above, these students learned to "think" of more variables at once, so they learned to make sense of the world in real time.

Amid the chaos of almost any class on a rainy day with a substitute teacher, I arrive for my weekly appointment with a fourth grade class at 1:25 P.M. I jump into teaching them how to represent fractions with movement. The students are thrilled to get out of their seats and move. The noise reaches an unbearable although predictable level, and in the middle of all this Andrés, as if saying "here, you can have it," hands me the creation he has spent all day realizing: a series of seven origami birds with the smallest nesting inside the next one, nesting inside the next one, nesting inside the next one. I marvel at the treasure and say so he can hear me over the noise, "Why don't you give it to the substitute teacher." "I did, and she just said okay." I guess this was not a very exciting response.

I identify with Andrés, of course. We're accomplices in the same joyful crime. We know this treasure is more than a "feat in dexterity," more than "proof of spatial intelligence," more than "self-expression." It is all of the above, but it is also a way of reaching, of saying "here, save this jewel before it gets destroyed. It has important secrets and I made it." I felt I was given Borges' Aleph (the point in space that contains all the other points), the secret of how things work, and he and I appreciate it. It also expresses how we feel as we go inside ourselves and discover layer after layer of complexity within, or as we go outside ourselves and discover we are in the middle of layer after layer of complexity in the world.

Of course, Andrés' origami is full of math. There is pattern, measurement (all by eye), shapes, fractions. He was able to see pattern at the different levels of folding. These patterns involve the recognition of shapes (triangles, squares, triangles within squares, and squares within triangles, and all of them within rectangles within the initial square piece of paper). It was the result of a lesson I brought the previous week in which we saw how from a square piece of paper emerges a life form that can be a bird, a dragon, or any other animal the imagination can conjure up and direct the hand to decorate. The minuteness of his figures astonished me— all the miniature puppets worked mechanically the way they're supposed to. The beak, which is a kind of a pyramid, opens vertically. The head, the body, and two wings are triangular in shape. For the beak to open and close, on has to hold the bird by its two wings, with fingertips touching the head, and press inward.

I later learn from someone who has tested Andrés that he might have some challenges in paying attention. He's easily distractible and would do better in a classroom with fewer distractions, I am told. It is interesting to think that he might have used this as a coping mechanism for adverse circumstances (rainy day, substitute teacher), but also that the artwork is even more significant precisely because of the situation in which it was created.

When I studied with guitarist Pepe Romero, I once asked how to concentrate on the music when one has many other worries in life. His answer was, "at home, when everyone is discussing, talking and stressed about something, I pick up the guitar and start playing." We don't know concentration and focus without their opposites, lack of focus and distraction. It is important to see, therefore, that for many children from other cultures and languages, adapting to an English-speaking world will be stressful and that artistic expression might be the appropriate medium for taking some control of the environment.

Thus, Andrés found a way to focus and calm down, take control of the situation, and express himself by making puppets; he demonstrated how he could go inside himself before jumping to fractions through movement. I too jumped into the activity after having taken a glimpse through that door that opened briefly.

As students find themselves and their way, they unknowingly show me the way, too. Art is the common ground they have with their English-speaking peers and with the adults around them. This applies to me too, as I navigate the waters of a different country and culture. Art is the great meeting space where we find ourselves and explain the world and our place in it to each other. Just as the origami birds open their beaks to let our voices be heard, our accents enjoyed, our colors admired, and the taste of our words savored, so we share each other's ways of naming the world. For me, this is the significance of the gifts children present to me. I receive them as the red rose receives red light out of the spectrum of white light and reflects it for our eyes to see.

Andrés was able to overcome three limiting forces working against him. First, his attention problem, bordering on ADD, was under control when he found a way to calm down and focus on the project. Second, he solved a great mathematical puzzle through making the puppets, thus overcoming his teacher's impression of him as a low achiever. Finally, he overcame the difficulties entailed in navigating the terrain between his cultural background and his new cultural milieu. The completion of this project produced in Andrés a great deal of pride and empowerment. But perhaps most importantly, Andrés experienced a great deal of joy and playfulness in making of this project. Joy and playfulness, of course, are not quantifiable categories of achievement, but they are nevertheless very important in education. These are the experiences that set off sparks in our students and set them on their way for a lifetime of learning.

## *Reference*

Koestler, A. *The act of creation*. London: Hutchinson, 1964.

# Teacher Change in Professional Development: Impacting Teachers' Culture through the Arts

**Tom Bennett**

---

### KEY CONCEPTS

- Educational reform
- Providing opportunities to students to question, experiment, and discover
- Curiosity and genuine learning
- Teachers' culture
- Artist culture
- Creative thinking and the arts
- Where the artistic process and teaching intersect
- Risk-taking
- Shifts in affective and cognitive beliefs and practice
- Assessing student learning

---

*The research reported in this chapter was assisted by a joint grant from the John D. and Catherine T. MacArthur Foundation and the Spencer Foundation under the Professional Development Research and Documentation Program. The data presented, the statements made, and the views expressed are solely the responsibility of the author.*

> Teaching is so constant within our own culture that we fail even to imagine how it might be changed, much less believe that it should be changed. (Stigler & Hiebert, 1999, p. 103)

Current educational reform efforts are pushing teachers to reconceptualize their practices in the hope of improving learning for all students (see, for example, National Council of Teachers of Mathematics, 1989; National Research Council, 1996). A consistent theme that runs through most reform documents is the call for teachers to provide students with rich learning opportunities that move them beyond the acquisition of basic facts and skills and toward the construction of strong content understanding.

In *The Teaching Gap*, Stigler and Hiebert (1999) suggest that because teaching is a "cultural activity," it is learned through participation in and observation of a culture over time rather than through formal study. For the purposes of this chapter, *culture* is defined as the beliefs, practices, and products that are shared by members of a group (Robinson, 1988). As participants engage in various events related to teaching, they form generalized mental pictures of that event, or scripts, that later help guide their behavior. For example, in mathematics the mental model of the scripts is based on four activities: reviewing homework, demonstrating how to solve new problems, practicing, and correcting seatwork, and assigning homework (Stigler & Hiebert, 1999). Scripts are widely shared within a culture and are often so entrenched in the culture of teaching that they are frequently overlooked (Stigler & Hiebert, 1999). Since teacher behavior is fundamentally guided by scripts, and since scripts are formed by observation and participation in a culture, if we truly want to improve teaching and student learning, we must find ways to improve teachers' scripts.

This chapter investigates the impact professional artists can have on teachers' culture when they collaborate with teachers to teach children core content through the arts. I describe how teachers' beliefs, practices, and products were impacted through their observation of and participation in the new classroom culture created through their collaboration with professional artists.

## Background

The primary driving force behind educational reform is to improve the learning of all students. To collaborate with teachers, members of an outside professional culture must have beliefs, practices, and products that will help teachers construct a classroom culture consistent with goals for student learning. In this section I consider how the culture of artists can help teachers create a culture that can lead to improved teacher practices and, ultimately, student learning.

The theoretical underpinning that motivates much educational reform today is that students learn best by constructing new understandings of relationships through goal-directed activities and exploration. Instead of learning facts through lectures, as students engage in a new task they assimilate new information according to their prior knowledge, thereby constructing their own meaning. Therefore, students must be provided learning opportunities that cause them to question, experiment, and discover relationships and facts (Ginsburg & Opper, 1988; National Council of Teachers of Mathematics, 1989). They must approach learning as genuinely curious individuals. Very young children, for example, approach the world this way. Because of their natural curiosity, they pick up objects, manipulate them, and inspect them closely in order to learn more about their properties. However, once children start school this kind of exploration often ceases (Ginsburg & Opper, 1988).

The artists' culture embraces exploration and investigation in the hope of better understanding the world. Artists are often naturally motivated to question, investigate, and explore an object or issue they want to express through the arts. For second language learners, this type of exploration is often not language based. For example, before Michaelangelo started sculpting *David,* he spent a considerable amount of time carefully studying human physiology to better understand the muscle and bone structure of the male human body. We might expect that the culture of artists can help teachers create a culture that encourages students to explore, investigate, and discover.

For children to truly learn, they must be mentally and physically engaged in the learning process. Applying Piaget's theory of intellectual development to the educational setting, Ginsburg and Opper (1988, p. 240) suggest:

> To promote genuine understanding, the teacher should therefore encourage the child's activity. When the teacher attempts to bypass this process in various ways—for example, by lecturing at a class of young children—the result is often superficial learning. Perhaps this is one reason why so much of what is taught in school is immediately forgotten after the school year ends. By contrast, genuinely active learning can lead to a more solid and long-lasting understanding.

To "do art," artists must be both mentally and physically engaged in the process. They must be mentally engaged when they consider what idea or concept to represent and what medium to use. Most of them must be physically engaged during the investigation, construction, and/or performance of their artwork. Therefore, we might expect that artists can help teachers construct a culture that actively engages students in the learning process.

Representing and communicating ideas, thoughts, and concepts in ways that can be shared with others is the essence of what teachers and students do in classrooms. In our current educational culture, the communication of thoughts and ideas typically occurs through the use of words and scientific symbols. However, many students are unequipped to effectively use words and symbols to express their understanding, especially when concepts are taught in linguistic terms. This is especially true of English language learners. In addition, many students use traditional forms of representation, such as symbols and procedures in mathematics, without understanding the mathematical concepts that are being represented. When this occurs, lack of understanding is masked; although the student might be able to correctly solve the problem using mathematical symbols, the representation is devoid of meaning. Teachers' ability to accurately assess students' understanding becomes severely limited. According to Hiebert and Carpenter (1992, p. 66), "the form of an external representation . . . with which a student interacts makes a difference in the way the student represents the quantity or relationship internally. Conversely, the way in which a student deals with or generates an external representation reveals something of how the student has represented that information internally." Teachers who want to better understand what students truly understand need to encourage students to use representations that convey meaning.

The artists' culture values expressing and communicating concepts, ideas, and thoughts using a wide range of different representational forms. Representations such as drawing, sculpture, music, theater, dance, and poems are media in which artists represent and communicate ideas, thoughts, and concepts (Goldberg, 2001). Often, these kinds of representations can provide greater opportunities for the more accurate expression of ideas and feelings not captured in words alone. Artists can meaningfully bring together ideas or concepts in a representation that can be communicated to and shared with others. Thus, we might expect artists to be able to help teachers create a culture that encourages students to use more meaningful ways to represent and express their understandings. Within this new culture, teachers should also be better able to make content more comprehensible

*Roxanne Kilbourne, SUAVE arts coach.*

to English language learners, and they should have more tools to assess students' understanding.

One of the big pushes in educational reform is to encourage creative thinking in students. We need students who can think creatively and solve problems. According to Piaget (1964, p. 5), "the principal goal of education is to create men [and women] who are capable of doing new things, not simply of repeating what other generations have done—men [and women] who are creative, inventive, and discoverers." Research suggests that 85 percent of kindergarten children are considered creative, but by the second grade this percentage decreases to a mere 10 percent of children (Barth, 1991).

A description of most artists is that they are creative and divergent thinkers. In addition to communicating ideas through the arts, artists often desire to invent new and creative ways to express their ideas and thoughts. We might expect artists to help teachers create a culture that promotes divergent and creative thinking by both teachers and students. This is especially important because one of the greatest challenges to the success of educational reform is to help teachers think about the teaching and learning process in ways that will reconceptualize their teaching in order to promote a deeper level of student understanding. For teachers to be successful at this, their thinking needs to be creative and divergent. We might expect that when teachers collaborate with artists, the artists help the teachers establish a new culture from which they able to develop more powerful teaching scripts.

We might expect the artists' culture in the classroom—more specifically, their beliefs, practices, and products—to assist teachers in constructing a classroom culture that is consistent with our goals for student learning. It is hoped their observations and participation in this new culture will encourage teachers to make fundamental changes in their culture.

Artists can have a profound impact on teachers' culture in ways thought to improve teaching and learning. Teachers' culture was impacted through (1) observation of artists' teaching content through the arts and their own participation in teaching, (2) observation of their students' learning as a result of being taught through the arts, and (3) the risk-taking process that allows teachers to put into practice what they have learned in their observations and participation. Before describing the kind of impact artists can have on teachers' culture, it is important to understand how the artists and teachers collaborate to prepare and teach children core content through the arts in the classroom.

## Factors That Impact Teachers' Culture

Artists can effectively impact teachers' culture in ways that are consistent with current reform recommendations. It is through observation of and participation in the artists' culture that teachers can make positive changes in their own culture. In this section I describe how teachers' observation of the artists teaching content through the arts, of their students' learning, and of the risk-taking process impacted teachers' culture in important ways.

## Observation of Artists' Teaching Content through the Arts

One of the factors impacting teachers' culture the most was their observations of artists teaching content through the arts and their own participation in teaching through the arts. Through the act of teaching, the teachers observed the artists' beliefs, practices, and products and were able to experience options for their classroom culture. Despite concerns that the artists might rely on the scripts they formed as students, the artists were able to reference their cultural beliefs, practices, and products as artists when teaching.

Teachers' observations of artists teaching can impact teachers' beliefs and practices in ways thought to improve student learning. For example, observations have helped teachers recognize the need for student exploration, experimentation, and discovery. This teacher describes how her observation of the artist helped her understand the importance of exploration and the need to push students to dig deep into the curriculum.

> I think [having the artist in our classrooms is] teaching ourselves to be freer to explore. Saying to a teacher it's okay to do—it is not a waste of instructional time, it's valuable time the kids need, no one ever taught us that. And it is through the artist coming in that we say "what is he doing, it is taking him two weeks to do this when I could have done it in five minutes"—but then maybe it wouldn't have meant anything to [the students]. First is the process that he took them through and now the kids really feel it. It is nothing that we could have read about or picked up from in-services or tips for teachers. It is by our own explorations and being with the coaches on a weekly basis that we have learned it is okay to take the time. It is not a rush rush curriculum. It is a cultural thing—it is a process rather than an end product. I don't want an activity-driven program, I want a process-driven program.

This teacher appears to be recognizing that her culture values quickly pushing through the curriculum rather than pushing for deep understanding and meaning through exploration. She also recognizes that she was able to learn this valuable lesson as a result of her active participation in the culture of teaching rather than through a book or in-service training.

Observations of their artist not only can impact teachers' beliefs related to teaching in more creative ways, but it can also push teachers to make significant changes in their practices. The following excerpt illustrates how one ESL teacher's beliefs and practices were impacted as a result of the artists' creative approach to the teaching and learning process.

> Just watching the way [the artist] moves has helped me to be freer in the classroom with my movement. He has so much energy and is just all over the classroom, the kids are just totally focused on what he is doing. And that has helped me to mimic some of that. In math we are doing area and perimeter and I started thinking "now how can I catch them with a story right off the bat?" . . . so I just started pretending I was this Army or Navy Seal type person, you know. The kids were like, "what is she doing?" you know, I wasn't saying anything. I was just really quiet, having all my men were behind me . . . and the boys were starting to jump out of their seats and go under their desks too and they were like the opposite. The only thing I said was "Okay, reconnaissance team, secure the perimeter." And they were like, "Oh!" And then I said, "What does that mean? We have heard that sometimes in movies." Then they gave me some ideas and then we started talking about perimeter and what that means and area. Watching [the artist] and the way he brings in all of his movement and expression has helped me to do something kind of crazy, but it gets the kids in an instant.

Artists have helped teachers reconsider the importance of the final learning product and to focus more on the learning process. The following excerpt helps illustrate how one artist was able to help a teacher alter her beliefs, practices, and products in ways that focus more on the process of learning rather than on the product that is created.

> And true learning, I think, is more process than product but at the same time, teachers get caught up in the product. I mean, I think we know that we've done a good job and we can show somebody that we've accomplished something when we have a product and it's all over and hang it up on the wall maybe, but the true learning really is the process, and like I said, one of the things with the artists is that we could create, and to me I think I grew up thinking you created something and then it was done, it was over, it was perfect or not perfect, but you left it alone. They never left anything alone. They kept coming back to it and adjusting or fine-tuning or tweaking or whatever, and to begin with, part of me went, "no, no, no, we're finished with that; let's just leave that," but in truth, I mean, that is the artistic process to go back and think about it and feel about it for a while and then go back and change it if you want to change it, or do it again but in a little different way. That was kind of new for me.

This example helps illustrate how the artistic process is compatible with how we want students to think about learning. Rather than having students think "I have learned that topic or concept," we want students to continue to revisit and reflect on what they have learned. When students are interested in learning about a topic, we want them to add new information to what they already understand, to continue to reconsider their ideas as new information comes in, and to believe that there is always something new to learn.

Engaging in artistic practices can also impact teachers' beliefs and practices in ways that encourage the active engagement of students in the learning process. For example, one teacher describes how her observation of the artist helped her teach a social science lesson in a way that actively engaged the students in the learning process.

> Until [the artist] started having us do movement to poems and things like that I hadn't thought of doing a social studies lesson this way. We teach about the land bridge, people coming across the land bridge to North America and becoming Native Americans. So I took a section of the playground . . . [and] had them act out the whole thing. And we slowly crossed the land bridge and moved down towards North America and then down to South America. We were chasing herds of animals and some of the kids were the mammoths. As we moved toward the equator we noticed it was getting warmer. I know that they are going to remember that. It wasn't just the two-page spread in the social studies book with a picture . . . of an Eskimo or whatever in furs and a bunch of words. . . . They acted it out, they moved, they walked, I talked to them the whole time.

The excerpts presented in this section help us better recognize the importance of providing teachers with opportunities to experience how the teaching and learning process can be different. In the next section we investigate the kind of impact teachers' observations of their students' learning can have on teachers' culture.

## Observation of Students' Learning

Since changes in instructional practices are based on the belief that they will positively impact students' learning, it makes sense that teachers benefit from seeing how these changes positively impact their students. SUAVE teachers regularly describe how they have come to realize that their students' learning is improved when they teach content through the arts. One of the most common realizations is how teaching through the arts can positively impact students who have not found success through traditional means. For example, the following excerpt illustrates how one teacher's observations of her students' learning impacted her beliefs and ultimately her practices in teaching special populations of students.

> When working in dual language instruction, [teaching through the arts] made it very visual and concrete for the kids. Kids have benefited from

it, I think. I have various RSP students that have benefited, special ed. students, bilingual kids learning a second language—I mean it is just so visual, so tangible for them to acquire and have access to the curriculum that it has made such a big difference in the way I teach. Everything is so tangible across the curriculum. I mean they can understand; they can see it, they can feel it, they can act it, they can say it.

In addition to recognizing the learning benefits of an active environment, many teachers have also noted that observations of their students have helped them to better understand the importance of student exploration. In the following excerpt, a teacher describes the level at which students can achieve when they are provided an opportunity to explore actively and represent their understanding in creative ways.

I can think of a couple of kids in my class that their reading comprehension has improved and I think a lot of it has to do with the different activities we have . . . [it] is just not the reading, but that they have been able to immerse themselves in whatever the content was. In science the other week we were reviewing the different movements of the water and each group was given a different movement [to present to the class], we did waves, we did surface currents or whatever. . . . I was just amazed at some of my lower kids and what they came up with. It wasn't just poetry, it was song, it was dance, it was acting and they really had the content areas and I was really impressed that in five minutes they could do that.

As illustrated in this excerpt, many SUAVE teachers learned that their students were not only able to learn effectively through the arts, but were also able to effectively represent and communicate their understanding through the arts. Finding ways for teachers to better determine what their students do and do not understand is important. The arts appear to provide teachers with an effective tool to accurately assess their students' understanding.

Teachers' observations of students engaged in learning through the arts have also impacted their culture related to affective concerns. Many teachers have noticed the way teaching through the arts can impact how students feel about themselves as learners, can give students confidence, and can make them happy. One teacher found that teaching through the arts promotes social justice and equity in the classroom by, for example, impacting the self-worth of a second language learner.

[Teaching through the arts] opens the floodgates of the second language, the gate that keeps them back, that keeps them limited and maybe questioning their own self-worth. It opens that gate because they have been actively involved and showing you they are feeling really good. It helps them so much to feel that, yes, I can learn this and I can do this because they had all of this great self-expression come out and they have been validated. I think that the self-esteem thing is such a powerful piece in the classroom.

Teachers' culture can be impacted in many positive ways when they are provided opportunities to observe students' learning through the arts. In the next section we investigate the impact the risk-taking process has on teachers' culture.

## The Risk-Taking Process

The risk-taking process allows teachers to put into motion all that they learned from their observations. In many ways, what teachers learned from observations of the artists motivated them to take risks in the classroom, and the risks teachers took allowed them to learn even more about teaching and learning through the arts from their observations.

The artists push the teachers to take risks when teaching in the classroom. Most teachers have reported feeling reluctant to teach an area of the arts, most often due to feelings of inadequacy. For example, some teachers described being reluctant to include music, dance, or drawing in their curriculum. However, teachers often described how the artists would help them move into areas they never would have explored without support and a push. The following excerpt illustrates how one artist was able to push a teacher to take risks in class while also modeling how to explore new areas that might be considered uncomfortable.

> [My artist] will push me to try things that maybe I wouldn't do and that's really a key. Also, she is willing to take chances, "Well I am not that strong in this area either but let's work together" and we are experimenting in areas even that we are both a little unsure of. So, I think a coach [artist] needs to be willing to take chances and also be willing to push, push me beyond my limits . . . which is the key to experimentation. . . . I am hesitant to do clay because it is quite a challenge for me. I haven't done that much of it so I have been sitting back and thinking "Well I do want to do that some day." [My artist] is trying to bring it in whenever we are discussing "we could do it this way or that way" and making it easier for me to experiment to put myself in that position that is a little bit more uncomfortable.

Some teachers have recognized that they must learn to take risks in order to make changes in their beliefs, practices, and products. Being forced to take risks helps some teachers find out more about themselves and move closer to their students. This excerpt helps illustrate the importance of the link that exists between the risks teachers take and their ability to assess the impact the risk has on their students.

> It was important for me to experience that I could do it and having the support of the kids—and they're so proud of you! And they said we never thought you could do that, so you come out of your shell and you discover yourself.

Sometimes the risks are not related to the arts, but rather to making changes in beliefs and practices related to teaching. For example, some teachers recognize the need to make changes in their teaching practices as a result of taking risks, even though the changes might be a little uncomfortable at first.

> I never wanted to be a clown in front of the class . . . my coach tells the kids "Now lets see [the teacher] do it" . . . it took me a long time before I could do it. Now I do it and I feel good about it and I really discovered that it is not that painful and the kids enjoy it. So, exploratory is wonderful!

Even well after the artists are no longer working directly with the teachers in their classrooms, SUAVE teachers suggest that they are still benefiting from the artists' encouragement to take risks.

Teachers' culture can be impacted in many positive ways when teachers are encouraged to take risks related to teaching students through the arts. It is one thing for teachers to observe how artists teach and the impact on students' learning. However, teaching students is much more difficult than simply recognizing good practices and successful approaches. For teachers to make real changes in what they do with students, they must be willing to take risks. If they don't take risks, education will continue to be stuck with the approaches that have endured for many generations.

## Creating Shifts in Affective and Cognitive Beliefs and in Practice

As teachers observe shifts in students' beliefs about themselves, they can also make important shifts in their beliefs about their students. Given the connection to the arts, we might have expected to find that teachers primarily observed shifts in students' affective beliefs. However, in SUAVE, teachers also made shifts in their beliefs about their students' cognitive abilities.

## Affective Beliefs

Teachers have recognized that teaching through the arts can have an impact on students' self-confidence, on their motivation to participate in class, and on their self-esteem and sense of self-worth. Many teachers report that their students respond more positively to learning when being taught through the arts. For example, teachers have commented that their students were more self-confident and more willing to take risks, leading to greater understanding, because many of students no longer felt they couldn't do the work because they didn't understand the material.

> I think in terms of subject matter knowledge it definitely intensifies and brings it to a level of comprehension and understanding by lowering the affective filter—where the kids feel that tension I can't participate because I don't know this.

Similarly, teachers have also reported that they now see their shy students taking a more active role in the class and in the learning process. Several teachers have found that when they provide their students with options to represent their ideas through the arts, some become more motivated to learn and participate.

> My shy kids have come to life; they feel that they are more a part of the community. When they go out there and I look at them and say "that cannot be that child, how come she is coming to life?" Otherwise she is sitting there totally quiet, she is never talking to anyone else. And because she doesn't have to necessarily speak . . . she is coming to life.

Because of their experiences with their students, SUAVE teachers continuously recognize the positive impact that teaching through the arts can have on students' self-confidence, motivation, and self-esteem and self-worth. One reason is that the arts provide students with options for representing and communicating their ideas in ways that are meaningful. This seems to be particularly true for second language learners and students not as comfortable communicating their understanding through the traditional means of written and oral language.

## Cognitive Beliefs

Teaching through the arts can impact teachers' views of students' cognitive abilities. Their experiences working with the artist and attempting to teach the content through the arts seemed to help teachers see students who were labeled as having lower ability as academically more competent. In SUAVE classes, students also began to see each other in new ways and recognize each other's talents.

A less able student academically who has a skill in music or rhythm or acting or drawing; other kids will go over to that person, who might have in past years been ignored or teased or just kind of pushed aside, I have students walking over and asking for help from different students during work times.

This excerpt helps illustrate how the artists can help teachers see their students as academically more competent. When teachers begin to see their students as academically more competent, their expectations also increase, leading to greater student learning.

# Changes in Teachers' Instructional Practices

Teachers involved in teaching through the arts often make significant changes in their instructional practices. More specifically, SUAVE teachers learned to engage their students mentally and physically in the learning process, to provide students with opportunities to explore, to create new ways for students to represent ideas and to create new ways to assess students' understanding, and to be less inhibited when teaching children.

## Learning to Engage Students Mentally and Physically

Teachers frequently comment that they have made significant changes in the way they engage their students in the learning process when they use the arts. They first consider how they might actively engage their students in the learning process when designing a lesson plan. The following excerpt illustrates how one teacher recognized the benefits of active engagement through the arts and, because of her experiences with her artist, is now more receptive to these ideas.

My mind is more open to trying things out through different modalities and presenting it to kids in a different way. So instead of finding out about fairy tales by reading, let's find out about fairy tales by miming them and then we will compare and contrast fairy tales. It is a different way of introducing things . . . it sounds silly but it gets the kids. You always worry as a teacher when you present a lesson, who are you leaving out, who is being excluded because you are presenting it one way. But I think with the arts you have a way of reaching everybody in some way, somehow. No one is excluded.

## Learning to Provide Opportunities to
## Explore, Investigate, and Discover

Teachers often see themselves as task oriented, and it took mentoring by an artist for them to (re)learn the importance of providing students with opportunities to explore, investigate, and discover. For example, the following excerpt from an end-of-year interview illustrates how teachers can learn to provide meaningful time for exploration and how this exploration can lead to a much deeper understanding of the content.

> *Teacher:* I am interested in students being able to look at a subject from a different angle. We are studying explorers, and to really get into the period we did some portraits of the explorers so they can really feel that these men were different, they were not just your dad or someone else, this was a different time period. By doing the drawing they were able to connect better to what they were learning about. It is putting more strength into the curriculum.

> *Interviewer:* So the connection then would be a connection between the content area and the art form . . . ?

> *Teacher:* And the students being able to express what they know through the art form too. They are kind of exploring the curriculum through the art and eventually showing what they know through the art sometimes too.

This teacher encouraged her students to explore the curriculum more deeply through the arts. She wanted her students to better understand who the explorers were, the time period they lived in, the kinds of clothes they wore. Teachers often initially feel uncomfortable providing students with time for exploration.

> It's definitely been a learning process for all of us in terms of allowing our students to explore . . . we [teachers] are so task oriented. Something else, not only does [the artist] give them exploration time, he also teaches them about self-discipline . . . and I see that self-discipline carrying over to other subject areas. He instills in them the importance of "yes it is okay to explore, but everything is done with a purpose."

Another SUAVE teacher learned that students need to be provided with opportunities to explore, and that this process takes time.

> You know what we know about good teaching is that you have to have the exploratory process before you give kids skills, especially in math.

> But I never connected it to the arts. . . . As teachers we didn't know the process took so long.

Although we might think the artist could support teachers only in ways related to the arts, both of these teachers commented that the artist also helped them better understand how students learn. These teachers learned that students need time to explore, and that this process takes time.

## Creating New Ways of Representing Ideas and Assessing Understanding

The coaching relationship has encouraged teachers to have students express their understanding of concepts in a range of meaningful ways through the arts. When students use these new representations, teachers often are able to more accurately assess their understanding. The following excerpt illustrates how teachers have made changes in their instructional approaches to encourage students to use meaningful methods to communicate their understanding.

> Worksheets have really disappeared from my classroom . . . now very rarely do we have a worksheet. They are doing it through all the other ways they can to express what they have learned or to practice what we are working on.

One challenge in teaching is accurately assessing students' understanding of the content. Often students memorize what they are told, but fail to really understand the concepts. Many teachers have commented that teaching content through the arts has provided them with new opportunities and strategies for assessing students' understanding.

> On the assessment side I have seen more of what my kids really are learning because of using the arts, visual and performing arts, as part of the assessment. You are seeing a true picture of what they really know, not what they are capable of writing or what they are capable of saying to you, but really getting a picture of what they know content wise.

Other teachers have found that when students learn and represent their understanding through the arts, teachers not only can better assess student understanding, but the students can learn more deeply.

> There are so many levels of learning. One of the deepest levels is when you have to turn it around and teach someone else. I have learned that art is just as strong as teaching someone because you can't act it out if you just half understand it. You can't draw a beautiful illustration if you

really didn't know what went on in the story so it made me realize that art can add to that depth.

## Final Comments

When we consider teaching to be a cultural activity that is learned through observation and participation in a culture, the challenge for professional development becomes providing teachers with opportunities that will impact their culture. When investigating the similarities between artists' culture and the culture we want teachers to create in their classrooms, it is striking how nicely these two cultures intersect. One of the benefits of SUAVE is not simply that it brings together artists and teachers, but that these two cultures come together and interact in the teachers' culture. For this collaboration to work, the teachers are forced to make accommodations for the artists' culture. The fact that the collaboration occurs in the teachers' culture seems to be a powerful component of SUAVE in helping teachers make changes in their culture.

Teachers' experiences collaborating with the artists in the classroom provided them with important opportunities to imagine how their teaching culture can be different. They were able to make changes in their beliefs about teaching, and with encouragement and some pushing from the artists, they were also able to take risks in their classroom to make changes in their practices. The opportunities to observe their students learning through the arts helped teachers realize the many benefits of teaching through the arts. It is difficult for teachers to not make changes in their beliefs, practices, and products when they are able to witness firsthand their students' successes.

Clearly, professional artists can have a major impact on teachers' culture in many important ways. In the context of the broader program, these results are particularly impressive when you consider that the artists often spent no more than one hour a week in teachers' classrooms over a two-year period. It appears that artists can contribute to society in ways that go far beyond their artwork. When artists are engaged in professional development programs like SUAVE, they can also play an important role in helping improve our educational system.

## References

Barth, R. S. (1991). Restructuring schools: Some questions for teaches and principals. *Phi Delta Kappan*, 73 (2), 123–128.

Ginsburg, H. P., & Opper, S. (1988). *Piaget's theory of intellectual development*, 3rd ed. Englewood Cliffs, NJ: Prentice Hall.

Goldberg, M. (2001). *Arts and learning: An integrated approach to teaching and learning in multicultural and multilingual settings*, 2nd ed. New York: Longman.

Goldberg, M., & Bossenmeyer, M. (1998). Shifting the role of arts in education. *Principal*, 77 (4), 56–58.

Hiebert, J., & Carpenter, T. P. (1992). Learning and teaching with understanding. In D. A. Grouws (Ed.), *Handbook of research on mathematics teaching and learning* (pp. 65–97). New York: McMillan.

National Center for Education Statistics. (1996). *Pursuing excellence: A study of U.S. eighth-grade mathematics and science teaching, learning, curriculum, and achievement in international context*. Washington, DC: U.S. Department of Education.

National Council of Teachers of Mathematics. (1989). *Curriculum and evaluation standards for school mathematics*. Reston, VA: NCTM.

National Research Council. (1996). *National science education standards*. Washington, DC: National Academy Press.

Robinson, G. L. N. (1988). *Crosscultural understanding*. Englewood Cliffs, NJ: Prentice Hall.

Stigler, J. W., & Hiebert, J. (1999). *The teaching gap: Best ideas from the world's teachers for improving education in the classroom*. New York: Free Press.

# 7

## *Forty Years of Teaching and We're Still Learners: A Practical Guide to Incorporating the Arts into the Curriculum*

**Karen Sleichter and Sherry Reid**
*Kindergarten and First-Grade Teachers*

*KEY CONCEPTS*

- Making learning come alive through the arts
- Strategies to reach ELL students effectively
- Examples of lessons in visual arts
- Thematic teaching
- Puppetry
- Music and compound words
- Involving parents

Teaching with and through the arts has been an adventure for us. We are compelled to take risks that sometimes lead to chaos and failure. Through trial and error we eventually achieve triumph and success. Being involved as mentor teachers in the SUAVE program has afforded us the opportunity to explore arts in a variety of ways in our classrooms. Collectively, we have over forty years of experience teaching various levels, grades, and classes. Our students have ranged from non-English to proficient English speakers.

As educators we are always seeking better ways of conveying subject matter to our students. In recent years we have been feeling the effects of imposed standards and grade-level expectations from our state and districts. This becomes a real dilemma when trying to incorporate everything into an already packed curriculum. Meeting the needs of students with multiple learning styles and respecting and incorporating the multilingual and multicultural backgrounds of all of students can easily go by the wayside when the demands to teach to tests interfere with education. It truly becomes a challenge, because we are caught between knowing and implementing truly effective methods for learning and meeting the demands from our districts to teach to frameworks, standards, and tests.

Our challenge has been to investigate a variety of methodologies to educate students who come to us with different academic needs. English language learners require even more consideration. Through our years with the SUAVE program, we

*Berta Villaescusa, SUAVE arts coach.*

*Karen Sleichter, SUAVE mentor teacher.*

have had an opportunity to work with artists on a weekly basis in our classrooms. Together, we collaborated on ways to teach the curriculum using the California standards and instructing through the arts. After observing and working with an artist, each of us made an important discovery: Using the arts as a vehicle for teaching is not only a highly motivating form of learning, but the subject matter becomes embedded in students' memories.

The arts help children use their bodies to explore essential elements of language. This is an integral part of instructing children whose first language is not English, and indeed also students whose first language is English. Children naturally use movement throughout their day. They play; they pantomime; they create hand-clapping games. The arts enable kids to utilize what comes naturally to them—movement—to process and acquire new language. Acting out a word, for example, can make it stick in the mind of a child who learns kinesthetically. Drawing the meaning of the word might help a visual learner. Applying new words to poetry might help a more logic-mathematical learner to apply the words. In all these cases, the children are actively engaged and working with language, rather than memorizing.

Movement, music, and chanting can be used as teaching techniques to explore curriculum and make it come alive. "Ranting," which is what we would define as a combination rap and chant, can be a wonderful tool for children. It enables students to apply language and use their creative abilities and provides an opportunity to apply their new skills in a mini-performance. The ELL student is brought to the same level as class peers in assimilating subject matter because he or she has an effective medium to apply new words. These are nonjudgmental techniques that show respect for every child's unique abilities and permit the self-concept of an ELL child to develop in a positive way.

A few years ago, one of our schools investigated a phonics programs that would meet the needs of our school and incorporate all the modalities of learning. The program, which we adopted and presently use, includes many elements of art—music, art, and movement. After using the program for four years, we discovered that ELL students retain letter sounds much better. This should not have been a surprise! The arts motivate the students and also give them concrete methods to retain words. For example, by seeing words in drawings or drawing the words in pictorial form, students better retain their meaning. Perhaps it is just that one is easily conditioned into viewing the arts as fluff rather than as essential in the process of teaching and learning.

Movement is a method of teaching that considers the development of the total child. Second language students are limited in conversation through spoken words. Using movement, however, allows them to act out words they are not yet ready to express orally. More often than not, after the experience of moving, ELL students are much more likely to use the language orally. It is if the acting out gives them the confidence that they do know the words and can use them. Using movement communication becomes a nonjudgmental way of expression for the ELL student and serves to preserves his or her self-esteem.

*Sherry Reid, SUAVE mentor teacher.*

A few key questions are crucial to any teacher working with multilingual students. We explored the following questions and asked them of our colleagues as we began preparation for this chapter.

- How do you reach (what are the most effective ways of reaching) second language students?
- Are there specific techniques that make curriculum more accessible to second language students?
- What are some examples this?
- How do you incorporate the arts in language arts, math, social studies, and science?

The following is a raw listing of the kinds of answers we brainstormed with our colleagues, all of whom have English language learners in their classes.

- Have kids perform.
- Sing it, act it out.
- When kids are not singled out and can do activities together, it brings down the fear factor. They participate on the same level with all kids; then you might have them do something independently.
- Show a real object, draw it, talk about it.
- Model by drawing.
- Put everything to music.
- Make a story come to life by having them act it out.
- Put concepts in simple tunes.
- Scaffold.
- Always remember the importance of hands-on.
- Encourage participation and make it safe to make mistakes.
- Be uninhibited—it makes learning fun, and kids will buy in.
- Take some risks that you haven't tried before.
- Be flexible, don't do too much in one lesson.
- Have other students explain concepts; sometimes simple language is better, and kids might do that better than us!
- Have parents work individually with students.
- Have kids show comprehension through the arts, picture drawing, and explaining with simple language.
- Use manipulatives such as flannel graphs and pictures to illustrate concepts.
- Act out concepts using full body movement.
- Use technology: computers to show comprehension, key concepts. Practice concepts through drawing illustration. Find out what kids are interested in in terms of technology and explore through a theme using the arts.
- Connect concepts through themes when possible. Sometimes kids will comment in an area where they feel more confident.

- Use a system of participation where every child gets a chance to participate (sticks, lotto balls, etc.).
- Create engaging routines.
- Do not be afraid of repetition.
- Encourage cooperative learning.
- Be aware of creating a nonthreatening environment.
- Always try to develop and incorporate nonverbal activities.
- When planning, think "step by step" as a process
- Consider what will enable a total physical response.
- Incorporate storytelling and puppetry.
- Integrate music as it can teach the rhythm of the language.
- Directed drawing gives students an opportunity to follow directions in a non-threatening way.
- Pay attention to incorporating the tactile into lessons.
- Make use of all the senses.
- Connect what students are learning to what they already know.
- Try to pull in writing with every art project.

Specific examples:

- To get kids to use adjectives in stories, toss a ball around in a circle. Keep adding adjectives to the sentences with every ball toss. This is a day. This is black day. This is a sad black day. A dog got lost. A brown dog got lost. A big brown dog got lost.
- Create (or have the kids create) a place value dance. In this activity, children create movements to signify single digits (such as clapping), tens (stomping), and hundreds (twirling). Children choose or are assigned a number and act it out through the movement.
- Create new lyrics to familiar songs to build vocabulary. Make a song about vegetables using "Old MacDonald Had a Farm." As each vegetable in the song is introduced, a real vegetable or picture can be held up by a child. Example: Mr. McGregor had a garden, ee i ee i oh. And in his garden he had a cabbage ee i ee i o.
- Use skip counting in math. Use songs to practice counting by twos, fives, and tens. Use rhymes such as two, four, six, eight, who do we appreciate? Consider adding new words to familiar skip rhymes.
- Create a history quilt (colonial). In this example, a class was divided into four groups of eight children each. The class researched and voted on the historical event they wanted to depict on the quilt. Each group decided which part of the picture they wanted to depict. The event that was chosen was researched. Each child then drew one-eighth of that portion of their group's picture. Everyone had to work together as a class and a group, and as an individual.

- Cook. Cooking involves hands-on measurement, fractions, and names of ingredients. It can become a terrific methodology, especially for mathematics.
- Act out events in history. Social studies becomes alive when students act out historical events as much as possible. This might be done after summarizing as a class, or as an introduction. Also incorporate drawing a picture and a written account of the event. This can be done cooperatively. Children often remember better as a result.
- Build science vocabulary. In science introduce familiar vocabulary like *stomach*, then add terminology like *abdomen*. Use what they already know in moving them forward. Always be hands-on; experimentation is fundamental as children try to remember and understand. Though books, paper, and pencil are important, always remember to make use of colors and the five senses (taste, smell, hear, see, and touch). All children identify things by their senses.

## Suggestions by Arts Discipline

This next section looks at the visual arts and performing arts and offers concrete suggestions on how to incorporate each into your curriculum.

### Visual Arts

Using the visual arts to teach the curriculum is an effective way to reach all students in a classroom, English learners as well as English-only students. As a student produces artwork, the student's understanding or lack of understanding of the lesson becomes evident.

One of our first-grade classes has been studying plant life for several weeks. As a culminating activity, each student creates an oil pastel drawing of a flower, including the flower, stem, leaves, and roots as they observe a live flower in a vase. The teacher guides them through each step of the pastel drawing, modeling the techniques as the children watch. The teacher removes the example, and the children draw their own flowers using the live flower as a guide. The teacher reminds them to include all parts of the flower. After their drawings are completed, each child meets with the teacher to discuss the drawing. The student explains each step of creating the flower and names each part of the plant. Together, the student and teacher labels the parts using computer-printed labels.

This art project becomes an evaluation in which the teacher measures a student's understanding of a plant and how well the student understood and was able to complete a multistep art project. Vocabulary development is also assessed as the student discusses the steps in creating the drawing with the teacher.

***Directed draw.***    When children first attempt to draw and color pictures, they sometimes experience difficulty in capturing what they want to show on their

## Parts of a Flower Lesson Plan

**Discipline Areas:** Science, visual art

**Goals:** Ability to recall parts of a flower. Follow a multistep art project. Drawing skills. Evaluate verbal skills.

**Materials:** Construction paper, oil pastels, live flower with roots attached.

**Procedure:**
1. Explain to students the object of the lesson.
2. Review parts of a flower, pointing to the real flower.
3. Demonstrate how to draw the flower with oil pastels.
4. Students draw the flower.
5. Teacher reviews parts of the flower as the students draw.
6. Student explains to teacher how the drawing was made and the names of each part of the flower.
7. Student labels the parts of the flower as teacher assists.

**Skills Taught:** Drawing skills, following directions.

**Assessment of Understanding:** Observe if all parts of the flower are included and labeled correctly; student is able to verbally explain the process of creating the drawing.

**First-Grade Standards Taught:** Life sciences standards; language arts listening and speaking comprehension; art; creative expression.

paper. We have found that the technique of directed art really helps children acquire the skills they need to begin to draw on their own. Children internalize the steps of a particular drawing, and it shows up later in their artwork. Directed drawing can be used to teach various subject matter. For example, every year in a study of the rainforest, directed art is used to teach about the various layers of the rainforest and the plants and animals that live there. As they learn about each layer, the children draw the animals in their natural habitat.

*Art-Based Thematic Teaching.* Thematic teaching—choosing a subject and developing curriculum around the subject—is a very useful form in the classroom. As a theme is carried through several areas of the curriculum, the lessons naturally develop into a complete picture. The student sees a connection in the subject matter as the theme is revisited in different areas of the curriculum such as language arts, math, science, and social studies.

## Directed Draw Lesson Plan

**Grade:** Kindergarten–second grade

**Subject Areas:** Language arts, art

**Goals:** Practice eye-hand coordination. Learn drawing techniques. Practice writing sentences that describe a drawing.

**Materials:** Paper, fine-line black drawing pens, crayons.

**Procedure:** The teacher draws on a paper using a step-by-step progression in completing a picture. The children then attempt to draw the same thing on their paper. This is done until all the steps are completed. The drawing can be colored after the directed portion is finished. Students write sentences to describe their drawings.

**Skills Taught:** Basic drawing, writing skills, following directions.

**Assessment of Understanding:** View pictures for accuracy; assess sentences for construction, grammar, and content. Check the extent to which the sentences match the drawings.

Through SUAVE training, we have found that using art as a beginning point for a thematic unit helps teachers develop lessons that cover many areas of the curriculum. Students show a high interest in the lessons and produce work that demonstrates their understanding. A thematic unit is usually taught over several weeks. The following is a format used to create a SUAVE thematic unit.

| *Format* | *Examples* |
| --- | --- |
| 1. Choose theme | Scarecrow |
| 2. Subjects to teach | Language arts, math, visual and performing arts, science |
| 3. Choose literature | Several stories about scarecrows. For example, *The Little Scarecrow Boy* by Margaret Wise Brown. |
| 4. Lesson plan | a. Introduce theme through literature. |
| | b. KWL chart. |
| | c. Teach life of a pumpkin. |
| | d. Create scarecrow art—pumpkin field and scarecrow. |
| | e. Measure dimensions of scarecrow. |

f. Students write or dictate about their scarecrow art.

g. Create a play about scarecrows.

5. Evaluation    Check for understanding as student completes each step of the lesson.

## Scarecrow in a Pumpkin Field Lesson Plan

**Discipline Areas:** Visual and performing arts, language arts, math, science

**Goals:** Understand growth of a plant. Watercolor painting. Story writing. Measurement. Perform in a play.

**Materials:** Construction paper for watercolor background and hat, straw, burlap for face (light brown) and two buttons for eyes, glue, scissors, scraps of material for scarecrow's clothes (orange material for nose), watercolors and paintbrushes.

**Procedure:**
1. Teach the life cycle of a pumpkin.
2. Read: *Jeb Scarecrow's Pumpkin Patch* by Jana Dillon (Boston: Houghton Mifflin, 1992) and *The Little Scarecrow Boy* by Margaret Brown (New York: Harper-Collins Publishers, 1998).
3. Paint background with watercolors—sky, background hills, pumpkin patch, fence.
4. Glue scarecrow's clothes and face (precut) onto dried painted background.
5. Trace hat, cut it out, fringe the brim of the hat. Glue onto head.
6. Stuff scarecrow's body with straw.
7. Measure height of scarecrow with ruler or yardstick.
8. Dictate or write a story about the scarecrow.
9. Whole class writes and performs a play about scarecrows.

**Skills Taught:** Watercolor painting, life of a pumpkin, measurement, follow multistep directions assembling the scarecrow, telling/writing a story with beginning, middle, and end, performing in a play.

**Assessment of Understanding:** Observe if all parts of watercolor background are included, scarecrow was correctly constructed, correct measurement, story had beginning, middle, and end, student can tell the development of a pumpkin from seed to fully grown pumpkin.

**Other Suggestions:** Teach more watercolor painting techniques, continue with measurement and story writing. Allow several days to complete the scarecrow project. Stuff scarecrow outside. Adults should cut out scarecrow's clothes. Total unit should be taught over several weeks.

## Performing Arts—Puppetry

Performing in front of an audience can be a frightening for a child, especially who is required to perform in a second language he or she is learning. Using puppe often reduces a child's fears and anxiety. To the child, it is not himself or herself speaking, but rather the puppet. The spotlight is not on the child but on the puppet.

Children learn many different skills when performing a play. They learn cooperation in working with other students. They learn to work as a team when they share lines. Language arts, reading, and speaking skills are enhanced from reading their lines and delivering them with expression. Their self-esteem is boosted when other students and their families watch them perform.

Puppet performances may sound time-consuming, complicated, and like a lot of work. During training in India with the SUAVE program, we were shown several forms of puppetry that can be used in the classroom. Some were very complicated, and some were very simple. One simple form is called "tabletop puppetry." As primary-grade teachers we have used this form of puppetry as an extension activity to a story the class read. A tabletop is used for the stage. A simple

---

### Puppet Play Lesson Plan

*Hattie and the Fox* by Mem Fox

**Materials:** Table, cardboard, construction and tissue paper, pipe cleaners, cotton balls, feathers, etc., for decorating animal puppets, glue

**Procedure:**
1. Draw outline of tree and hills on cardboard. Cut it out and cover it with construction paper and tissue paper.
2. Make animal puppet bodies with folded over construction paper. Attach heads. Decorate with various materials, depending on the animal. Example: cover sheep with cotton balls.
3. Print script for students to read, using large print.
4. Practice the play for several days before performing. Coach students on movement of puppets and expression when lines are read.
5. Perform for parents and other classes.

**Skills Taught:** Visual arts: constructing a puppet and background for a stage. Performing arts: acting a part out through puppetry. Language arts: reading and speaking with expression.

**Assessment of Understanding:** Ability to create a puppet. Ability to perform in front of an audience, speaking with expression at the correct time in the play. Cooperating with others as a member of a team.

**First-Grade Standards Taught:** Language arts standard listening and speaking; art, visual and creative expression.

tline of a tree and hills is covered with construction and tissue paper round. The students stand behind the table and work their puppets, n the table. The script is taken directly from the book. (For primary-, a simple text works best.) The teacher narrates the story. Depending e ability of the students, lines are assigned by level of difficulty.

## ...orming Arts—Music

We can all remember familiar tunes we learned as children. They stay with us throughout our lives. Putting concepts such as grammar and parts of speech to simple tunes helps children remember them. Here is an example of a lesson on compound words using music.

### Learning Compound Words through Music Lesson Plan

**Grade:** Second

**Subject area:** Language arts

**Materials:** Chart with song written in large print. Tape or CD of "Did You Ever See a Lassie," paper, a variety of art supplies

**Procedure:** This song on compounds is taught to the children after an initial introduction to compound words. When the children become familiar with the song, they can fill in the blanks with their own words. For example, "Did you ever see a drumstick, a drumstick, a drumstick, did you ever see a drumstick go this way and that." The words should be accompanied by movement. This technique is particularly effective with second language students. After a few days, the children can illustrate a compound word of their choice. Using a variety of art media to culminate this project adds high interest for the students and makes a nice class display.

**Examples of compound words:** Beehive, tapeworm, backbone, drumstick, nighttime, bookworm, eyelash, toenail, fingernail, keyboard, eyeball, basketball, football, baseball, toothbrush, toothpaste, raincoat.

## Involving Parents

To conclude this chapter, we want to encourage teachers and future teachers to inform and involve parents in what you are doing at school. Every year we send home letters describing our work. These letters are in both English and Spanish. Having the support of parents can become critical in achieving goals throughout schooling. Here is one example of our letters.

## Parent Letter

Dear Parents:

This school year, your children will be afforded a unique opportunity! I am currently one of ten teachers at Felicita who is involved with the SUAVE arts through education program. Every week, an art mentor comes to our classroom and works with me and my students to teach some area of the curriculum. Many varieties of art forms are used during these sessions, including music, drama, puppetry, art, and movement. Research has shown that children can more readily recall what they have learned using the arts. My students also receive a great deal of enjoyment from this method of learning. They always look forward to their SUAVE time.

Your child will be bringing art projects home throughout the year. Some of these projects take up to a week to complete and are directly related to our curriculum. Please talk to you student about his or her work, and display the results proudly in your home. I invite you to come and see one of our SUAVE sessions during the school year. If you have any questions, please feel free to call or stop by school.

Sincerely,

Mrs. Karen Sleichter

Queridos padres:

Este año sus hijos van a tener una oportunidad única. Actualmente soy una de las diez maestras en Felicita que está metida con el programa SUAVE que es un programa educacional a través del arte. Cada semana va a venir a nuestra clase un mentor que va a trabajar con mis estudiantes y conmigo en alguna área del currículo. Se usan una extensa variedad de formas durante estas sesiones, incluyendo: música, drama, títeres, arte y movimientos. Estudios nos demuestran que los niños pueden recordar más rápidamente lo que han aprendido usando el arte. Mis estudiantes reciben también un gran pacer en el aprendizaje de este método. Ellos esperan con entusiasmo el rato que pasan en SUAVE.

Durante todo el año, sus hijos van a llevar a casa proyectos de arte. Algunos de los cuales les tomará una semana para completarlos y están relacionados directamente con nuestro currículo. Por favor, hable con sus hijos sobra sus trabajos y expóngalos con orgullo en alguna parte de su casa.

Les invito a que vengan a ver una de nuestras sesiones de SUAVE durante este año escolar. Si tiene alguna pregunta, por favor llame o venga a la escuela.

Sinceramente

Sra. Karen Sleichter

# 8

# Experiencing Science through the Arts

**Victoria Jacobs, Merryl Goldberg, and Tom Bennett**

## KEY CONCEPTS

- Arts encourage language development
- Art-based assessment
- Art and motivation to learn
- Learning weather vocabulary through drama
- Learning about the water cycle through movement and music
- Learning about the solar system through music
- Learning about adaptation through drawing
- Learning about animals and their environments through origami and storytelling

*The research reported in this chapter was assisted by a joint grant from the John D. and Catherine T. MacArthur Foundation and the Spencer Foundation under the Professional Development Research and Documentation Program. The data presented, the statements made, and the views expressed are solely the responsibility of the authors. An earlier version of this chapter was presented at the 1999 annual conference of the American Educational Research Association in Montreal, Canada.*

### Grade 2: Experiencing Life as a Bat

*The second-grade classroom is darkened, like a cave. The children sit on the floor, anxiously waiting to find out who will be chosen to play the baby bats and who will become the mother bats. Six children are identified as baby bats. Each baby learns to make a unique clicking sound with his/her tongue and is given an odor (a cup containing a banana, an apple, vinegar, a chocolate cupcake, nontoxic paint, or soap). Six mother bats are blindfolded, and each is paired with a baby to learn her baby's specific clicking sound and odor. It is time for the drama to begin. The mother bats go out of the cave to find food. During this time, the baby bats rearrange themselves and line up to represent a small group of the many baby bats that hang upside-down in a cave waiting for their mothers to bring back food. One by one the mother bats return to the cave and try to find their babies using only sounds and odors as clues.*

After this drama, this teacher commented that she felt that her students finally understood what it meant to be a night creature and how a bat moved through the darkness using only sound and smell to find its baby. In the past, this teacher felt that she had talked about these concepts, but the students had never *experienced* them and, therefore, never really understood them. Six months after this drama activity, students still talked about finding their babies and could even recall the odors they had used to identify those babies.

Students in these SUAVE classrooms did more than study animals. Rather, they became those animals and actually experienced life as the animals might. What makes these classroom scenarios so powerful? The arts have long been known to deeply connect people with ideas and emotions (Dewey, 1959; Greene, 1991). However, arts in elementary schools have often been separated from the core curriculum and offered instead as enrichment activities that are considered beneficial but not essential. These two scenarios provide examples of how the arts can be integrated with other subjects, such as science (the focus of this chapter), to teach the core curriculum. This is in contrast to the more traditional form of arts education in which the goal is to teach the arts themselves. Goldberg (2001) highlights this distinction by contrasting teaching *about* the arts (traditional disciplined-based arts instruction) with teaching *through* the arts (using the arts as a teaching strategy to help students understand content other than the arts).

Teaching through the arts requires students to engage in the act of creating art. For example, they might draw pictures, write poems, act in dramas, or compose music to further their understandings of concepts in content areas other than the arts. Teaching through the arts helps students *experience* concepts rather than simply discussing or reading about them. This approach is consistent with educational theories that highlight the importance of reaching multiple learning styles or intelligences (Gardner, 1993). As one SUAVE teacher explained:

## Grade 4: Experiencing Life as an Animal

*The fourth-grade class is preparing to produce a play about nature in which the students will portray animals like tigers, coyotes, and rabbits. Students are working in groups to create short scenes with animals and some type of action. Some of the students will play animals, and others will serve as musicians playing instruments. The animals will use actions but no words. The musicians will dictate the pace of the scene and changes in the action with changes in their music. Students begin performing for each other. The teacher reminds the students, "Anyone can put on a costume and look like a cat, but you need to act like a cat. Your personality needs to take on the animal's personality." This session is the first time the children have tried to "become" animals. Many of the scenes are short, with children giggling, and the action is usually restricted to chasing each other.*

This is the beginning of several lessons designed to use drama to help students improve both their observation skills and their understandings about animal characteristics. Rather than providing students with elaborate costumes and props, the teacher wanted students to "become" their animals. In a subsequent lesson, she had students study animal characteristics by viewing videos about animals and their habitats. Students were also assigned homework that required close observations of the mannerisms of a pet or other animal. In another lesson, students learned a Brazilian dance, *capoeira*, to help them move more like animals and less like children. The teacher also created a "magic carpet" activity to help students move beyond their silliness and become their animals. The magic carpet was a rectangle of floor space marked off by yarn. When students stepped into the magic carpet, they became an animal with all of its characteristics, actions, and so on. When students stepped out of the magic carpet, they were children again. This delineation helped students focus on portraying their animals with appropriate characteristics, movements, and intentions. Over time and through participation in these types of activities, students' understandings and performances improved.

The other thing that's come . . . from SUAVE—I've always had it but SUAVE really taught me how to tap into it—is that every child experiences things in different ways. Those learning modalities are critical in my opinion. But before, it was such a laborious job to figure out how am I going to tap into all of those different learning styles. SUAVE has made it natural, so every single week when I sit down and plan, I think about SUAVE techniques/twists and I put in this lesson what will tap into those different learning styles. To me, that's how I'm reaching kids that I may have missed in the past.

The use of the arts to address different learning styles has been particularly effective in multilingual settings. Written and verbal language barriers often seem to disappear when the arts are involved. The arts become a new language that students learning English as a second language can use to communicate (Gallas, 1994;

Goldberg, 2001). First, the arts become an important instructional technique for learning content and developing language. As one teacher explained, the arts are "a form of expression," and this form of expression "makes language bubble out." An example of how the arts can encourage language development comes from a particular student with language difficulties. His teacher explained:

> The student has difficulty turning his assignments in for science class, partly for personal reasons, but mostly language reasons. The student speaks English, but can barely read or write it. The Magical SUAVE Moment occurred while integrating art and science. The objective was to draw a cell through a microscope, label cell parts, and write a reflection, "How shape of cell is related to function of that organism." Well, it turns out this student is an extremely talented artist, and was able to write a reflection piece of equal quality (of mind) because it was his cell drawing. The student has since turned in all the cell labs on time. Art has bridged the language/content gap!

Second, the arts become an effective assessment technique, particularly for students with language barriers. As the following teacher explained, art-based assessments often provide more accurate information than traditional assessments.

> A lot of times my kids who are lower in language—I find out how much they know about what we've been studying [by using the arts] . . . I am amazed like sometimes they'll draw something and I'll say, "Well, tell me about that." And they say, "Well this is this and [so on]" It's like

*Mindy Donner, SUAVE arts coach.*

"Wow" . . . but if I had them write it out on an essay test, there's just no way that it would show . . . [art is] a way for them to express what they have learned and validate that, yeah, [they] do know what [they] are talking about.

Teaching through the arts also has the potential for providing other benefits traditionally associated with the arts. Specifically, the study of the arts has been linked to students' increased critical and creative thinking skills, self-esteem, willingness to take risks, and ability to work with others (Gallas, 1994; Goldberg, 2001). Risk-taking is something that SUAVE teachers have consistently mentioned both in terms of themselves and their students. One teacher described how SUAVE helped her learn to value risk-taking:

[SUAVE] gave me the courage to take risks. . . . Push yourself. See what else you can do. Don't be afraid to succeed. You know most of us are afraid of failing. Well if we don't do it, we fail. But if we do it, there's no failing there. . . . [SUAVE has] given me that attitude that as a teacher, do something, step out on a limb. See if you fall or if you fly. I don't know. I think it's kind of helped me take flight . . . I'm going to try more stuff.

This teacher also explained how she modeled risk-taking for her students by participating in artistic activities that are uncomfortable for her, and she reflected "I think the kids are changed . . . because like me, they're less afraid to try something artistically." This teacher and others recognized how risk-taking in the arts often translated into risk-taking in other areas of a student's (and teacher's) life. For English language learners in particular, risk-taking becomes an important life skill because of the daily risks involved in learning a second language.

Similarly, success in the arts can build a child's self-esteem in both the arts and life in general. Many teachers talked of the value of giving all children the opportunity to "shine," and for many children who struggle academically, the arts are the only arena that provides this opportunity. One teacher described how a child who hated school is now choosing to stay after school because of his involvement with the arts:

Here's a kid who struggles with writing and reading and math and all these subjects . . . . and I think that's why he acts up so much in class . . . But I tell him all the time, "you're an artist." And he has really neat stuff . . . . art's like the one thing that he can sit down and really do. He could do it for two and a half hours and not get into trouble.

The teacher paid the $15 fee for the child to enroll in an after-school arts program. Not only did the child attend, but he chose to sign up for an additional sculpting class. Another teacher recognized the importance of the arts in building the self-esteem of a student who was identified as GATE (gifted and talented) but who also had very low English skills. The teacher explained, "I think the art and the expression via the arts has made her just much more open. Just much more open and comfortable with herself and more comfortable with her peers."

Finally, teaching core curriculum through the arts introduces children to the arts themselves. Given the shrinking budgets of school districts around the country, arts specialists and arts programs have disappeared from many elementary schools. Teaching through the arts provides teachers with a means of using the arts successfully and in a way that is not just one more thing they must include in the curriculum. Rather, as one teacher stated, teaching through the arts is "accomplishing the same goals and the same tasks, but in a better way." At the same time, students are exposed to the arts as worthwhile disciplines in and of themselves.

The goal of this chapter is to highlight how, with proper teacher guidance, teaching science through the arts can help students more deeply understand scientific concepts. Specific examples were selected to depict lessons of different lengths with a variety of scientific concepts, art techniques, and grade levels (1 to 5). The examples also show different uses of teaching through the arts. For example, arts can help introduce a topic to students and/or help them review information they have already been studying. Finally, this set of examples was chosen to illustrate some additional benefits of teaching through the arts such as engaging and motivating students, reaching all students (including some who have been unsuccessful), and introducing students to the arts themselves. All of these examples were drawn from SUAVE classrooms in San Diego county.

## Grade 1: Learning about Weather Vocabulary through Drama

The teacher taught weather vocabulary by helping students use drama to express and interpret their understandings of the words. The focus was on vocabulary that the class had previously identified in weather-related literature, such as *frost, rainbow, sunny,* and *cloudy.* Each word was listed in a pocket chart next to drawings the children had already created to depict the meaning of the word. All the words were removed from their pockets, shuffled, and placed into a hat to be picked. Students were divided into pairs, and each pair picked a word that they needed to discuss and decide how to depict in a dramatic scene. To help others understand the meaning of their word, students were allowed to use actions and sounds, but no words. The rest of the class then tried to guess the word based on the students' dramatic presentation.

For example, two girls showed *shade* by having one girl sit on the ground with the other girl leaning over her with arms outstretched and fingers wiggling. The students were able to guess the word *shade* by recognizing the standing girl as a tree offering shade to a sitting girl. They also recognized the tree by her leaves (fingers) blowing in the wind. In another pair, two boys showed two depictions of the word *blow*. First, one boy puckered his lips and blew as hard as he could, and the second boy pretended to fall over. At this point, the other students guessed *windy*. Next, the boys both blew really hard to make the American flag in the room move back and forth. With this clue, the other students were able to guess the correct word, *blow*. This example shows how the activity not only helped children gain an understanding of the target words, but also highlighted related words such as *wind* and *blow*. Finally, two boys showed their understanding of *warm* by using their knowledge of its antonym, *cold*. The boys began their skit by shivering in the cold. They then moved themselves inside by a warm fire and began drinking hot chocolate. The processes of creating and interpreting these presentations helped deepen students' understandings. The teacher saw such growth in the students' understandings that she continued the activity with a new set of vocabulary words in the following lesson. Students also overwhelmingly agreed that they enjoyed the activity and thought it was a good way to study their vocabulary words.

## Grade 2: Learning about the Water Cycle through Movement and Music

The teacher taught the water cycle through movement and music by helping students experience the cycle over a series of lessons. First, the students were informally introduced to the water cycle as part of a series of activities to help them understand snowflakes, the focus of their poetry lesson. In order to "experience" being a snowflake, students listened to Tchaikovsky's *Nutcracker Suite* (the "Waltz of the Snowflakes") by closing their eyes and visualizing themselves as snowflakes on an adventure—beginning as a water drop, turning into vapor, condensing, and then shattering and falling to the ground as a snowflake. The students were asked where they landed after their adventure, and the responses included landing on a tree, in a Jacuzzi, in the mountains, and on somebody's head. The teacher also shared her adventure in which she landed on the eyelash of a deer.

The students then listened to the music again, this time acting out the water cycle (the snowflake's adventure) with movement and dancing. The teacher even continued the playacting by integrating the ideas into her classroom management. For example, she asked the students to go back to their desks as snowflakes flying and twirling. Through these inviting introductory activities, students began to develop an interest in the water cycle. The motivational powers of the arts are significant, as the teacher explained: "Hooking a kid is half, if not more than half, the battle of learning. If you can hook them then you can get them to learn."

In subsequent lessons, the teacher more formally introduced the water cycle by identifying and explaining the stages of accumulation, evaporation, condensation, and precipitation. The students then created a "sound sculpture," making different sounds (pounding on the floor, snapping, rubbing their hands) to represent each stage in the water cycle. Students played the four stages in order, over and over again, to reflect the cyclical nature of the water transformations. Some students then developed movements (twirling, freezing) to correspond with each stage. Others were given "instruments" (bottle, umbrella, wastebasket) to develop a new set of sounds. The performance was repeated multiple times, with some students moving while others were making music. The teacher eventually challenged the musicians to move beyond four sounds by asking them to incorporate different rhythms and speeds.

The teacher kept the students focused on the scientific concepts through her questioning and use of proper vocabulary. She did not tell the students which sounds or movements to use, as substantial learning occurred through this creation process. Rather, she pushed students to think deeply about their sound and movement choices, as these choices reflected their understandings of the scientific concepts. She asked general questions like "What does accumulation mean?" and "What might accumulation sound like?" She also challenged students on some of their choices. For example, students initially rolled themselves into balls to indicate accumulation (as in water droplets in a pond). The teacher expanded their understanding of this stage beyond water droplets that are motionless by challenging them to create sounds and movements that reflected water droplets rolling downstream in a river or stream. Similarly, when students were all using the same sound for rain falling, she challenged them to discover different sounds that reflected how we hear rain differently when it falls on grass, cars, people's heads, and so on.

## Grade 3: Learning about the Solar System through Music

The teacher taught the solar system by helping students create music to review and deepen their understandings of information they had already been studying. Specifically, groups of three to four students worked together to develop lyrics that reflected their understandings of Earth, the moon, and/or the sun. The new lyrics were to be sung using familiar tunes such as "Row, Row, Row Your Boat" and "Twinkle, Twinkle Little Star." Initially, the class jointly brainstormed many of the relevant scientific facts and concepts that they knew. After writing this information on the board, students broke into groups to decide on their topic, brainstorm possible sentences to include, and compile the sentences to match their assigned tune. For example, one group created the following lyrics to be sung to the tune of "Row, Row, Row Your Boat":

### Moon Moon in the Sky

*Moon Moon in the Sky*
*What are you made of?*
*I am made of dust and rock*
*And I have craters too.*

Another group created lyrics for "Are You Sleeping":

### The Moon

| *(Verse 1)* | *(Verse 2)* |
|---|---|
| *Moon has phases.* | *Waxing waning.* |
| *Moon has craters.* | *Waning waxing.* |
| *Yes it does.* | *Moon is new.* |
| *Yes it does.* | *Moon is full.* |
| *It is without gravity.* | *When it's new it can't be seen.* |
| *It is without atmosphere.* | *When it's full it shines bright.* |
| *Nothing lives.* | *Pretty sight.* |
| *Nothing lives.* | *Awesome sight.* |

In order to create these lyrics, students needed to discuss their understandings and convince others in their group of the facts they wanted to convey. For example, one group debated whether the moon had a small amount of gravity or no gravity at all. Another group recognized that a song about the moon should not include references to day and night since those concepts involve the moon but actually apply to Earth. Other students explored relationships between concepts when, for example, they needed to find synonyms so that a concept would match the assigned tune. The teacher kept the students focused on the scientific content by asking questions such as "What is your song teaching us?" Throughout the activity, the textbook was available for students to refer to and use for additional information. Students also reviewed concepts and clarified understandings by listening to other students' presentations.

In addition to scientific content, the teacher helped students gain an appreciation for lyricists and their profession. She drew from the students' recent experience of watching the 1997 Academy Awards, in which music from the movie *Titanic* won the award for best song. The teacher explained:

> Think about James Horner. He was the man who wrote the music to *Titanic*, and he also wrote the song. This is just real basic what we're doing here. We're trying to tie in some of what we know, our knowledge of the moon, into some songwriting. And taking songs that we already know and we're just plugging in facts that we know about the moon. But think about a songwriter like James Horner who wrote that music and had absolutely nothing to really go on other than his experience and his expertise. And now you really can feel the excitement that he must have had being chosen [at the Academy Awards] among all of those incredible musicians. . . . So you understand the difficulty in songwriting. Every time you listen to a song, you should really appreciate the fact that somebody probably didn't get a whole lot of sleep at some point in time!

# Grade 4: Learning about Adaptation through Drawing

The teacher taught the concept of adaptation through a drawing activity in which the students had to apply their knowledge of adaptation to create a new species of fish.[1] Students were divided into groups, and each group was given a different set of four adaptation cards. The cards indicated the (1) mouth (e.g., sucker-shaped, elongated upper jaw), (2) coloration (e.g., striped, light-colored belly), (3) body shape (e.g., torpedo-shaped, humpbacked), and (4) reproduction (e.g., floating eggs, live birth). For example, a group might receive cards that indicated that their fish must have a sucker-shaped mouth, striped coloration, vertical disk-like shape, and live birth for reproduction. The teacher also provided each group with an information sheet describing advantages and examples of the adaptations. For example, for the flat-bellied fish, the information sheet identified the advantages of this body shape (the ability to bottom feed) and provided examples of fish with flat-bellied body shapes. Students were asked to be creative in designing their fish and its environment. They could create their fish as flat (by drawing) or as three-dimensional (by drawing and then using items like beans or beads). The only requirements were that their fish needed to contain the four adaptations described on their cards. The students acted as scientists, even calling themselves "Doctor." After designing their fish, each group created a scientific name for it, making sure the name was consistent with the four adaptations.

Students reviewed concepts and deepened understandings by having to discuss what characteristics to give their fish. For example, one group discussed whether it was sensible to give a wide tail to a fish with a torpedo-shaped body. They eventually recognized that a wide tail on a torpedo-shaped body would negate one of the main advantages of this sleek body shape: speed. The teacher commented that this approach "allowed them [students] to go ahead and see relationships better . . . it really caused them to focus on those adaptations." The creative process pushed students to understand the adaptations and their advantages. This activity was also particularly motivating because it followed a class visit to an aquarium.

# Grade 5: Learning about Animals and Their Environments through Origami and Storytelling

The teacher reviewed animals and their environments by having the students develop and present stories of origami creatures that they invented. Initially, students were guided through the steps that were necessary to make an origami creature, and then were given the opportunity to decorate the creature any way they

---

[1]This activity is based on the "Fashion a Fish" activity suggested by Project WILD (1992b).

wished. Students learned quickly and not only made more creatures of the same size, but also figured out how to make creatures of different sizes, thereby creating "families" of creatures. This lesson was initially a mathematics lesson based on paper folding, but the creatures were so motivating to the students that the teacher decided to extend the lesson to science as a review of previous work on understanding animals and their environments. She explained to the students, "You can't just create a creature and have no life form . . . every person, every living thing has a story to tell." Each student was then invited to tell a story about his/her creature. The teacher reflected on this activity:

> We didn't sit there and discuss . . . you need to include this and you need to include that. I just said it had to be from the animal kingdom and you had to be aware of their environment and somehow put that into your story. But they were real creative . . . Some of them used personification. Some of them were very scientific and factual . . . And I had so many kids participate. I was just figuring that one or two people would get up there but they all wanted to get up!

The teacher was impressed both with the content of the students' presentations and with their eagerness to participate—even those children who were shy or typically did not participate. She specifically noted that "a lot of the kids that turned out to be experts with origami were the kids who normally struggle in class academically, so that's always a nice change." Teaching through the arts is often motivating and effective in making the lesson accessible to all students. In doing so, teachers are often able to see their students in new ways:

> I think that's probably one of the greatest things about art. You find out who your kids really are. I mean, my real quiet ones turn out to be some of my best artists. . . . If we weren't bringing [the arts] into the classroom I would never see that side of the child, and I'd always have this [limited] view. But now I have a complete picture. . . . It's like a little treasure that you don't even know that you're looking for, and then they come out.

## Conclusion

In addition to introducing students to the arts themselves, these examples show the power of the arts as a teaching strategy for various scientific content. Many of these activities are similar to ones recommended by Project Wild (1992a, 1992b), a well-respected science program that outlines interdisciplinary activities to help K–12 students develop awareness, knowledge, and skills related to the environment and its conservation. Some of the other Project Wild activities that involve the arts include

- Creating murals depicting the three major stages of pond succession
- Acting like herds of animals seeking food to learn about carrying capacity (the number of living things that can be supported by an area of land and/or water)
- Brainstorming water words and writing poetic statements about them to learn about the importance of water to people and wildlife

It is notable that science programs are promoting similar types of arts integration activities to learn *science* content. The arts can help students experience, and therefore more deeply understand, concepts in science and other core curriculum areas. Whether used as an introduction or a review technique, the arts have the power to motivate and engage students, even those who are traditionally unable or unwilling to participate fully in school lessons. In particular, students who are learning English benefit from the multiple forms of communication that the arts provide for their ideas. In addition, teachers and students enjoy teaching and learning through the arts. However, integrating the arts into an activity does not guarantee that a lesson will be effective. Teachers play a critical role in highlighting scientific content so that the curricular goals of the lesson do not get lost. Nonetheless, with proper teacher guidance, the arts can become an engaging and effective instructional technique for helping students learn science and other core curriculum.

## References

Dewey, J. (1959). *Art as experience*. New York: Capricorn Books.

Gallas, K. (1994). *The languages of learning: How children talk, write, dance, draw, and sing their understanding of the world*. New York: Teachers College Press.

Gardner, H. (1993). *Frames of mind: The theory of multiple intelligences*, 10th anniversary edition. New York: Basic Books.

Goldberg, M. (2001). *Arts and learning: An integrated approach to teaching and learning in multicultural and multilingual settings*, 2nd ed. New York: Longman.

Greene, M. (1991). Texts and margins. *Harvard Educational Review*, 61 (1), 27–39.

Project WILD. (1992a). *Project WILD K–12 activity guide*. Houston, TX: Council for Environmental Education.

Project WILD. (1992b). *Project WILD aquatic education activity guide*. Houston, TX: Council for Environmental Education.

# 9

# *Uncovering an Artistic Identity While Learning to Teach through the Arts*

**Victoria Jacobs, Merryl Goldberg, and Tom Bennett**

*Reprinted from* Passion and Pedagogy, *Peter Lang Publishers*

*KEY CONCEPTS*

- Artistic identity
- Teacher as artist
- Social learning and the arts
- Teaching philosophy and the arts
- Learning artistic techniques and activities
- Personal development in the arts
- Risk-taking

*The research reported in this chapter was assisted by a joint grant from the John D. and Catherine T. MacArthur Foundation and the Spencer Foundation under the Professional Development Research and Documentation Program. The data presented, the statements made, and the views expressed are solely the responsibility of the authors.*

> So if we are open to the idea that art is any form, any way of expressing ourselves, then . . . everyone has the ability to be an artist. And I think everyone is an artist. It's just up to the audience. It's up to the rest of the world to figure out what form of art they are excelling in.

This quote comes from Rita, a fifth-grade teacher in her fourth year of a professional development program focused on incorporating the arts into the curriculum. The quote reveals beliefs that are quite different from her beliefs when she began the program. Rita's initial view of the artistic community was that art was restricted to a select and talented few. She identified particular students in her class who were the "artists." She also specifically stated that she was *not* an artist, especially in comparison with several members of her family whom she described as artistically talented. After her experiences in the program, Rita felt that she now belonged to that previously exclusive artistic community. While she did not view herself an expert, Rita's identity now included her artistic self. Rita recognized that she had learned how to think like an artist, take risks like an artist, and believe in herself as an artist. She said that the program had forced her to reach *within herself* and take the "art out of my brain." She acknowledged an emerging view of herself as an artist: "I may not know what my talents are, but . . . if I'm able to express myself then I'm an artist and I think I've found different ways to express myself." This admission reflected her broadened view of the arts as "another form of communication" and an artist as anyone who "finds a new way to express themselves."

This story reflects learning at a profound level. Through her participation in a professional development program, Rita uncovered a new (artistic) identity for herself. Educators have long struggled with the goals and format of professional development opportunities for teachers. Typical programs involve "one-shot workshops" aimed at helping teachers learn a particular technique or activity that they can immediately use in their classrooms (Sykes, 1996). This story suggests that professional development programs have much greater potential. The chapter uses Rita's voice to explore the uncovering of her artistic identity, which included both professional and personal growth. First, however, the chapter describes the professional development program that focused on helping teachers like Rita learn to teach through the arts. It also introduces a theoretical framework that conceptualizes learning as the process of (re)forming identities.

SUAVE provides multiple learning opportunities for teachers (Bennett, Jacobs, & Goldberg, 1999), and teachers have specifically underscored the importance of the following:

- Personalized, sustained coaching in their classrooms
- In-services in which teachers have the opportunity to share with teachers from other schools and engage with professional art and artists as both *learners* and *audience members*
- Connections between the in-services and classroom coaching such that teachers have support to try (in their classrooms) what they have learned at the in-services

- Other teachers at their school sites who provide both support and motivation to teach through the arts (since each school site includes ten participating teachers)

SUAVE does more than provide teachers with opportunities to learn. The program also creates an atmosphere of excitement, encouragement, and resources that promotes widespread participation and a feeling of being professional and a part of something special. Teachers are treated as professionals in many ways ranging from being invited to sit-down lunches during in-services to having opportunities to interact with world-renowned artists to the program philosophy that is based on the idea of synergism between two professionals.

Rather than a traditional coaching model in which the coach would be the "expert" and the teacher a "novice," SUAVE views teachers as an integral part of successful classroom coaching. While coaches bring professional knowledge about the arts (e.g., techniques, creativity, multiple modes of communication, a curiosity for exploring the world, etc.), teachers bring professional knowledge about teaching and the students in their classroom (e.g., curriculum knowledge, classroom management skills, age-appropriate expectations, rapport with specific students in that classroom, etc.). These two players then collaborate to design lessons that teach core curriculum through the arts. These lessons are customized for a particular topic and particular students (vs. a prescribed curriculum). They are also designed so that they are appropriate for the comfort level and ability level of the teacher and coach involved. Each player has his/her own expertise and motivation, and their collaboration, which takes place in a noncompetitive, nonthreatening environment, often creates instruction that is substantially better than either player feels capable of producing alone (Bennett, Goldberg, Jacobs, & Wendling, 1999).[1]

## Learning in SUAVE

Wenger's (1998) social learning theory provides a useful lens for examining teacher learning in SUAVE. Wenger conceptualizes *all* learning as identity development:

> Because learning transforms who we are and what we can do, it is an experience of identity. It is not just an accumulation of skills and information, but a process of becoming. (Wenger, 1998, p. 215)

Wenger views this "process of becoming" as a social process, one that involves participation in the practices of a community. These communities are

---

[1]The data for this chapter were drawn from two years of data including fifteen classroom observations, multiple interviews, written evaluations, and focus group discussions. This case study specifically examines Rita's second and third years in SUAVE, and all quotes reflect her voice.

plentiful, can be formal or informal, and exist in all facets of life (e.g., workplaces, schools, families, hobbies, etc.). However, communities are not just groups of people defined by some attribute such as gender or ethnicity or location. Rather, the term *community* reflects a group of individuals with a dense web of relationships and shared meanings. As such, SUAVE is a community composed of teachers, coaches, the program director, and various support and research personnel. Members share the program philosophy of teaching through the arts and, over time, have developed multiple layers of interpersonal relationships, common experiences, and shared understandings. Within the SUAVE community, there are also many subcommunities reflecting individuals' goals, talents, responsibilities, and so on.

Individuals can belong to multiple communities simultaneously, and through their participation in these various communities, they can develop multiple identities. The development of multiple identities becomes an important goal for education given Wenger's conceptualization of learning as identity development. Wenger also claims that this goal will be achieved most effectively by providing learners with opportunities to participate in meaningful activities with others in the community. This approach, when applied to professional development, suggests that teachers should be actively engaged in the practices of a community rather than being informed about techniques. SUAVE's program design is consistent with Wenger's ideas. During both in-services and classroom coaching, SUAVE teachers are engaged in the practices of the artistic community. They participate as teachers, learners, and audience members.

Wenger also recognizes that helping learners to engage with current practices is not sufficient. Rather, education should also help learners explore "who they are, who they are not, who they could be" (Wenger, 1998, p. 272). Exploring "who they could be" involves the use of imagination to envision what is possible. Support for this exploration is perhaps SUAVE's greatest contribution, and for many teachers, an unexpected benefit. Teachers typically join the program with the hope of integrating the arts into their professional lives. They want to learn artistic techniques and activities as well as an understanding of when and how to use the arts in the classroom. SUAVE helps teachers gain this knowledge and more. In addition to supporting teachers as they incorporate the arts into their professional activities, SUAVE helps teachers grow personally. They often learn to engage in and value the process of risk-taking, a process inherent in most artistic endeavors. Furthermore, many teachers discover and are surprised to find artistic talent in themselves. The incorporation of the arts and the artistic process into teachers' personal lives is intertwined with the integration of the arts into their professional lives. SUAVE encourages both of these processes and helps them converge in a way that lets teachers uncover their artistic identities.

The rest of this chapter presents a case study describing what one teacher gained while learning to teach through the arts. First, the chapter will describe Rita's growth as she incorporated the arts into her professional life. Changes in her teaching philosophy and the increase in her knowledge of artistic techniques will be explored. Second, the chapter will acknowledge how Rita incorporated the arts into her personal life. Her adoption of the artistic process of risk-taking as well as her discovery of artistic talent within herself will be addressed.

# Incorporating the Arts into Rita's Professional Life

The uncovering of Rita's artistic identity involved professional growth on multiple levels. First, Rita reexamined her teaching philosophy to clarify and strengthen her beliefs about the role that the arts should play in education. Second, Rita learned about artistic techniques and activities so that she could more easily incorporate the arts into her classroom.

## Reexamining Rita's Teaching Philosophy

Through her participation in SUAVE, Rita reexamined and revised her teaching philosophy. The arts were no longer just a special treat; the arts had become a core component of her teaching:

> I'm constantly doing art and I don't even realize it anymore. . . . It's just part of the curriculum now, instead of just a special thing. . . . It's a treat in the fact that it's art, but it's not just this once-in-a-while thing. It's just part of the curriculum and now I don't even look at it as separate.

Specifically, Rita refined her use of the arts in the classroom and deepened her belief in the value of the arts as a teaching and assessment tool.

***Refining Her Use of the Arts in Classroom.***   SUAVE helped Rita extend the purpose of her arts activities beyond providing students with a "fun" experience:

> [SUAVE] makes me think about how much art I'm doing and it makes me think about why I'm doing the art to make sure I'm getting something out of it instead of just having fun. I used to do that, I used to do—"OK, this will be really fun for the kids"—and that's how I would decide what kind of an art project I would do. But I think more about it now; there's more of an educational background to what I'm doing. . . . And by that I mean I really think about the curriculum and what can the kids get from this and how will it help them with this subject or with the theme or whatever it is I'm trying to teach them.

By using her arts activities to enhance learning in core curriculum subjects, Rita grew to embrace the program philosophy of teaching *through* the arts. Rita described how she often used the arts as a culminating event, one that "extends what you're learning or it ties it all in together." She also used the arts as a motivator to "get them excited about learning something, to get them to want to learn."

***Valuing the Arts as a Teaching and Assessment Tool.***    The arts inherently elicit and support multiple ways of knowing and learning in contrast to the more traditionally limited school approaches. As such, Rita grew to value the arts as an effective teaching tool that could satisfy different learning styles so that *all* students had an opportunity to learn:

> I talk to the kids about this. I said, "Well if I just showed you this way, how many of you would get it?" And I do something, and I do that one way, and maybe a third of the hands will go up. . . . And then maybe fifteen minutes later, same situation. "OK, if I just showed you this way , how many of you would get it?" You have maybe another third raise their hands, you put it away and do something else. Fifteen minutes later I'll say, "What if I showed you this?" And then do it. More kids will raise their hands. Some of them are the ones who raised their hands earlier, but then when I do a combination, every kid raises their hand and says "Oh, I can do that." And I think, oh that's teaching . . . and that's hard to do sometimes . . . That's what [the coach] and I used to do last year. We really tried. "OK, how else can we teach this?" We have the acting or the dancing or shadow puppets or drawing or painting—trying to do as many different ways because not every kid's going to learn the same way. And I thought if you just expose them to different ways, everyone will eventually get it.

Rita also noted that the arts were an effective assessment tool as they gave her more accurate pictures of students' understandings than traditional assessments. For example, in an arts-based lesson on character analysis, Rita reflected on the importance of the artwork of one student who was getting all Ds and Fs academically:

> So here was a way—if I had given her a test, she probably would have failed it. If I had asked her to write a paragraph, or five paragraphs, she probably wouldn't have gotten the main idea, but *through her art*, she could give me—that was her way of showing me all the information that she gleaned from that.

Using the arts as an alternative form of assessment frequently had an additional benefit of allowing different groups of students to excel. Students who were academically low, shy, or difficult behaviorally were often the ones who excelled in art. Rita valued these surprises as "it kind of balances the class out." Rita also valued the arts as an assessment tool because it helped her to view students more holistically, sometimes revealing talents that she (and they) may not have known existed:

> I think that's probably one of the greatest things about art. You find out who your kids really are. I mean, my real quiet ones turn out to be some of my best artists. . . . If we weren't bringing this into the classroom I would never see that side of the child, and I'd always have this view. But now I have a complete picture. . . . It's like a little treasure that you don't even know that you're looking for, and then they come out.

## Learning Artistic Techniques and Activities

Learning artistic techniques and activities was an important component of the professional growth that led to the uncovering of Rita's artistic identity. The possibility of learning these techniques and activities was the main reason why Rita initially joined SUAVE:

> When I first started SUAVE I thought that somebody was going to come in and teach me techniques. . . . I really thought [the coach] was going to come in and say "OK, today we're going to do this and this is how you're going to do it," and then when she left, I was going to be able to use it the next week, and every week she was going to teach me something different.

At some level, Rita was initially disappointed that the weekly coaching proved to be more of a partnership. In other words, the coach did not have or give all the answers. This format was unfamiliar given the traditional transmission model of most professional development opportunities for teachers. Therefore, even though the program was not structured as she expected, Rita was still inspired to find these "techniques" elsewhere. For example, Rita enrolled in art classes on her own. Similarly, at in-services, Rita frequently chose to attend sessions with artists who gave her step-by-step instructions. Throughout the program, Rita often reflected on her (and other teachers') desire and expectation to learn a multitude of artistic techniques. The program did help her learn these techniques although not always through the direct instruction approach she had expected. Nonetheless, when reflecting on her experiences, Rita acknowledged the value and effectiveness of the program design. In SUAVE, teachers are encouraged to *participate* (with support) and as such, are able to take more ownership over the learning that occurs.

> We [Rita and other teachers] were actually disappointed at first, because we kept thinking "So when are they going to come in and teach us these great techniques?" and that's what we were expecting. . . . You think it's going to be a directed art lesson, sort of directed to me, as the teacher.

But I'm looking back and I think I'm glad it wasn't that way because now I can take ownership on what we learned . . . and I'm more comfortable. . . . I feel like I probably learned more this way than if they had said "OK, this is what you're going to do. You're going to do A first, then B, then C."

Rita's artistic growth is particularly evident when examining how she improved her existing lessons. For example, Rita created an arts-based lesson to help students understand character analysis of the novel *Guests* (by Michael Dorris). Specifically, she wanted the students to tell her, *through their art*, "how a character grows and evolves and changes throughout the story, and what causes those changes." Students were asked to create four mini-dioramas that were combined to form a pyramid. The first scene included the book title and a representation of the major theme of the book. The remaining three scenes depicted the evolution of the main character during the beginning (scene 1) , middle (scene 2), and end (scene 3) of the story. Before participating in SUAVE, Rita had used a similar activity when her class was studying friendship and reading the novel *The Wind in the Willows* (by Kenneth Grahame). When she described how she had modified this initial lesson to create the activity for *Guests,* many of her changes reflected her new knowledge and confidence about art. For example, she felt better able to help students understand the difference between two-dimensional and three-dimensional art:

> The first time, the kids just drew and pasted on the back wall of their pyramid, but this time I said, "OK, remember 3-D." And I showed them the difference between two-dimensional things and three-dimensional things and I said "this is how you make it real. . . . Everything you do you have to remember there's shape to it. You have to think—How thick is this? How thin is this? What does it look like if I'm looking at it from here? What does the back angle look like?"

Similarly, she felt better able to help students show character analysis through facial expressions and, in particular, through the eyebrows:

> We talked about eyebrows . . . and that's something I've been trying to teach them with trying to do portraits—you have to really pay attention to the eyebrows. If you're going to show anger, these are the ways that angry eyebrows go. If you want to show surprise, they're shaped like this—and that's something I got out of SUAVE.

Rita learned these artistic techniques and activities through her weekly coaching, the in-services, and the outside art classes in which she enrolled. Examples of her learning from each of these sources are described below.

***Learning Music through Coaching Sessions.***  Rita was partnered with a coach whose specialty was music. Rita was delighted that this pairing would give her an opportunity to expose her students to music—an area in which she felt limited:

> I've always been a singer. I can't read music—I mean, I can read music enough to go higher, lower, hold it or take a breath, but that's not really reading music. It's getting by, and I wanted to do something more for my kids. . . . I mean, I can put a tape in, "OK, we're going to sing this song," but that's not teaching music. So when [the coach] came in, I thought "OK, this is it. I know what I'm doing. Here's a great opportunity to give my kids something that I can't offer them."

During the year, her coaching included many musical activities such as making instruments out of household items, creating music with these instruments, playing conventional instruments, listening to music, singing songs, and so on. The students enjoyed and learned through their musical experiences. Rita also learned about music and gained the confidence to include music in her future classes, even without the support of a coach:

> Now I can really teach them something about music and OK, so I'm still not going to be able to teach them how to read music very well . . . but I can work with instruments and I can tell them the type of instruments and I can tell them why they're that [type of instrument], and they can learn all of that. I could not have done that [before SUAVE].

***Learning Portraiture through In-services.***  The in-services were particularly fertile ground for learning techniques and activities. During these sessions, teachers acted as students while working with artists on various art projects. Rita consistently praised the in-services as a valuable resource for teachers:

> Every time we have an in-service, we learn at least three different activities, and they're activities that we can use. And whoever teaches them, they obviously teach them well enough that we feel comfortable enough to do it, without the coach. . . . I think that speaks for itself.

In many cases, the in-services pushed teachers to engage with the arts in ways that were unfamiliar to them. For example, Rita was surprised and delighted that she learned how to draw a portrait of Martin Luther King. She learned about different views (e.g., profile, front view, etc.) and tips to make sure that facial features are proportioned properly. Rita chose to share her own drawing with her students, and then help them to create their own portraits of Martin Luther King.

***Learning Mask Design Through Art Classes.***  Rita's supplemental art classes often focused specifically on learning techniques such as using watercolors or colored pencils. During one class, she learned about a particular mask is made by using only scissors, paper, and glue. Rita then chose to have her students create these masks as a "getting to know you" activity during the first week of school. Her experiences creating masks also gave her the idea that other projects might benefit from restricting the possible materials (as was done in making the masks). This idea proved fruitful in multiple projects and she explained that "it seems like the less I give them, the more they give me back."

## Incorporating the Arts into Rita's Personal Life

The uncovering of Rita's artistic identity also involved personal growth on multiple levels. First, Rita learned to value risk-taking both in her role as a teacher and in other areas of her life. Second, Rita learned to believe in her own artistic talents.

### Learning to Value Risk-Taking

The artistic process is inherently risky, dependent on both exploration and experimentation. As Rita learned to appreciate risk-taking in the arts, she also found value in using the same approach in other areas of her life:

> [SUAVE] gave me the courage to take risks. . . . Push yourself. See what else you can do. Don't be afraid to succeed. You know most of us are afraid of failing. Well if we don't do it, we fail. But if we do it, there's no failing there. . . . They've given me that attitude that as a teacher, do something, step out on a limb. See if you fall or if you fly. I don't know. I think it's kind of helped me take flight . . . I'm going to try more stuff.

Initially, risk-taking during coaching sessions was safe for Rita because she had a coach who could assist her if things went awry. However, even without a coach, Rita said that she still felt the "spirit" of risk-taking. Rita credited both the classroom coaching and the in-services with helping her develop this spirit of risk-taking. Being encouraged, supported, and even pushed to participate helped Rita recognize qualities in herself that she did not know existed:

> A positive about having an art coach is one, if you're going to fail, you're not by yourself . . . and then in-services—because you're surrounded and they make you do things, they make you participate, things that— oh my God if you had asked me to come up with a chant . . . there's no way. But you're with your colleagues. You're with one of the coaches. You can do this. It's a team effort and it turns out to be a good thing.

During her three years in the program, Rita took many risks ranging from drawing a portrait and sharing it with her students to learning how to be more relaxed about a messy room and running overtime. Rita acknowledged that risk-taking is not always easy but SUAVE has given her the courage and desire to try new things. It has also helped her recognize that there is still value in trying something that does not work out exactly as planned:

> I also try to do things that I'm not so comfortable with, and that's really hard for me because I don't like change, and sometimes I'm afraid of change. . . . But SUAVE has kind of given me—it's almost like a safety net. . . . Even though I don't have the coaches with me anymore, I still have kind of that spirit and it's like—OK, so if it doesn't work out, you're still going to get something out of it.

### Believing in Rita's Own Artistic Talents

Through her participation in SUAVE, Rita grew to better understand and value the arts in both her professional and personal lives. Perhaps most powerful was her recognition of artistic talents within herself—talents that she initially denied existed:

> I can do a lot more than I thought. I actually have more artistic talent than I knew. . . . like with the sculpting and just working with clay or doing a mural—three years ago, I would never have done any of this.

Finding the artist in herself helped Rita recognize the necessity of nurturing the artists in her students—and helping them recognize the artists in themselves.

> That is something SUAVE gave me . . . to remember or just be more aware that kids truly are artists, and it's up to me to find out what means they're going to use to express themselves . . . And if I don't do that, I'm never going to know what my kids can really do . . . I say, "Rita, push yourself so you can push your kids, and you can be surprised with what they can do."

Just as Rita was surprised with the extent of her own artistic talents, she was continually surprised with what her students were able to accomplish.

## Conclusions

Rita's story underscores the potential of professional development programs to help teachers change at a profound level. Wenger's social learning theory provides a framework to help push professional development programs beyond simply transmitting techniques. By viewing learning as the development of identities, more profound growth is possible and probable. Rita's story provides evidence that professional development programs have great potential to help teachers learn through the uncovering of new identities. However, in order to accomplish this goal, programs need to be (re)structured to support participation in meaning-ful activities with others (rather than a transmission of instructional techniques). Through participation in the artistic community (with support), Rita came to rec-ognize, nurture, and value the artistic part of her identity. She joined the program with the intent of improving her professional activities, but instead found a new (artistic) identity that influenced both her professional and personal lives. Rita's story also reminds us that the power of the arts is not limited to students' learning (Catterall, 1995; Gallas, 1994; Torff, 1994). Rather, the arts can also be a powerful catalyst for teachers' learning.

> It's kind of a reminder—hey, you know what? Art is here and it's shaped our world in so many ways and it's not going away. And you can take it out of our classroom, but we're going to find a way to bring it back. . . . Because you know other people see art as fluff-fluff or fu-fu, and I'm thinking NO. If you can tie it in with what you're learning, and if you can make this art somehow make it alive and have whatever you're learning come alive in the classroom, then it's not fu-fu and it's not fluffy stuff, it's education. It's learning. It's real, and isn't that the whole point of education?

## References

Bennett, T. R., Goldberg, M., Jacobs, V., & Wendling, L. (1999, April). *Teacher learning in professional development: The impact of an "artist as mentor" relationship.* Paper presented at the 1999 annual meeting of the American Educational Research Association, Montreal, Quebec, Canada.

Bennett, T. R., Jacobs, V., & Goldberg, M. (1999, April). *The power of multiple learning environ-ments in professional development.* Paper pre-sented at the 1999 annual meeting of the American Educational Research Association, Montreal, Quebec, Canada.

Catterall, J. S. (1995). *Different ways of knowing: 1991–94 national longitudinal study.* Los Angeles, CA: Galef Institute.

Dorris, M. (1994). *Guests.* New York: Hyperion Books for Children.

Gallas, K. (1994). *The languages of learning: How chil-dren talk, write, dance, draw, and sing their under-standing of the world.* New York: Teachers Col-lege Press.

Goldberg, M. (1997). *Arts and learning: An integrated approach to teaching and learning in multicultural and multilingual settings.* New York: Longman.

Goldberg, M. R. & Bossenmeyer, M. (1998). Shifting the role of arts in education. *Principal, 77* (4), 56–58.

Grahame, K. (1966). *The wind in the willows.* New York: Grosset & Dunlap.

Sykes, G. (1996). Reform of and as professional development. *Phi Delta Kappan, 77* (7), 465–467.

Torff, B. (1994). *Evaluation of Wolf Trap Institute for early learning through the arts.* Cambridge, MA: Harvard Project Zero.

Wenger, E. (1998). *Communities of practice: Learning, meaning and identity.* New York: Cambridge University Press.

# 10

# The Mirrored Selves as Once Echoed by Duke Ellington: Practicing and Professional Development

**Merryl Goldberg**

*Music isn't something that can come "unglued from a sheet of music. . . . and you want to know if I still practice? That's the least I can do for what I've gotten. As my doctor once told me, 'I haven't arrived; I practice medicine.' Me too. I haven't arrived. Just making the trip daily."*

Art Hodes (in Gottlieb, 1996, p. 66)

**KEY CONCEPTS:**

- Practice and practicing
- Risk, at-risk, risk-taking
- Brainstorming
- Trust and confidence
- Support
- Flexibility
- Attention to the possible
- Culture of invention

*The research reported in this chapter was assisted by a joint grant from the John D. and Catherine T. MacArthur Foundation and the Spencer Foundation under the Professional Development Research and Documentation Program. The data presented, the statements made, and the views expressed are solely the responsibility of the author.*

This chapter is in essence about practice—practice that takes place weekly among artists who work on a day-to-day basis with elementary school teachers. It concerns itself with the complexity of "vague and misty overtones" witnessed as reflections in a mirror, according to one jazz musician, and with the nature of risk in understanding what is possible, according to another.

You have now read about the SUAVE program and its impact on teachers learning to integrate the arts throughout the ELL curriculum. A key aspect of SUAVE, and an element that sets it apart from other programs, is the role and importance of the weekly two-hour "coaches meeting." Every Tuesday from 3:30 to 5:30 the coaches (now numbering twelve) meet with me (the program director) at the Center for the Arts in Escondido. We share experiences, brainstorm activities, and solve problems. Coaches meetings also serve as an environment for learning about art forms, art techniques, and classroom activities. This occurs through sharing successes as well as failures or mistakes in developing ways to work with teachers or involve them more (being "sneaky," as we like to describe it).

## About Practice

You might be wondering what this has to do with practice. In order to be proficient at the piano like Art Hodes, a well-known jazz musician who played with Louis Armstrong and Bessie Smith, one needs to practice. To practice implies honing skills, learning new repertoire, studying interpretations, perhaps creating ideas for

*Kim Emerson, SUAVE arts coach.*

improvisations or compositions. In visual arts, practice is also an aspect of the creative process; artists often keep sketchbooks to try new ideas, or develop paintings by doing a series on the same theme. As Vernon Howard (1991) so aptly put it, practice is far from "the drudgery of drill." Rather, practice at its best includes inquiry, discovery, and assessment. This sounds remarkably similar to a great classroom atmosphere in terms of encouraging children's learning.

Practice can, and often does, include experimentation and reflection; it is an action or a verb, as Howard reminds us, not only a noun. As a reflective activity, practice may start as looking into a mirror and beginning with what one sees. A teacher might pay attention to what the child first sees as she or he begins looking at her or his reflection. As practice deepens, the musician may use the mirror as a pondering tool. The child may use the mirror to question what is or what is possible. If one looks deep enough, the mirror might reveal possibility, or even defeat. Fortunately, I believe, most artists and children tend to embrace possibility, and employ defeat as a tool for the future rather than as a hindrance.

Musical ensembles practice together. The practice sessions are not necessarily to get ready for performance, but to become better musicians or to keep invigorated. For example, jazz musicians will often get together to "jam." Jam sessions provide space and time to improvise, try out new compositions, explore new arrangements. The musicians take risks inventing solos, new harmonies, background counter-melodies, and so on. They think about each others' improvisations and "riffs"—phrases they will play while others are improvising. During jam sessions it is not unusual to make sure each person is getting the notes right. But usually this is the least important aspect of a practice session. The real work is in finding the music—creating an interpretation, learning to work with each other, playing off one another as if the ensemble were one musician instead of a group of people playing together. The participants are present to what is happening. This work is far from mindless. Its outward simplicity shades the complexity that requires creative and critical thinking and reflection, concentration, listening, responding, and reacting.

The artists of SUAVE are practicing and experimenting with their art forms; they are involved in professional development in the realm of the arts. The work and atmosphere of the coaches meetings can offer insights into an ideal classroom for not only ELL learners, but for all learners.

Coaching meetings provide practice—in the form of a jam session. Improvisation in the same areas as the jazz ensemble—creative and critical thinking, reflection, concentration, listening, responding, reacting, and risk-taking—is key to the process. Jam sessions are a way of being for musicians and also for the coaches. They thrive on the sessions, on improvising, on trying things they have never tried before, what others might call risk-taking.

All practice sessions begin with the surface, a look in the mirror. "Art is a mirror of life" and "art imitates life" are common notions of the function of art in experience (Goldberg, 2001).

What interests me about the mirror metaphor is that it incorporates the notion of reflection. If art is a mirror of life—which I believe art can be—it necessitates reflection. And in that reflection we often see things that are or aren't there. Our look is discriminating. The same is true of our look at life; it is discriminating according to our experiences, culture, gender, environment, and so on. Art enables us to see things that are both there and not there; it provides us with an opportunity to imagine and reflect on our lives. (Goldberg, 2001, p. 9)

In preparing this chapter, I became very interested in the mirror notion when I came across the writing of a well-known jazz musician, Duke Ellington (1973, p.451). Ellington wrote a poem where he ponders the reflection we see of ourselves as we look into a still pool of water and see ourselves reflected back. What is it we really see, who are we? We look at our "wonderful selves-of-perfection" and revel in its delight. However, as we look deeper into the pool, we realize there are reflections beneath the surface, in fact there are many reflections below the surface. Who are the people just underneath the surface? Do we know these people, do we like them, do we celebrate them? Each reflection adds more depth and perhaps uncertainty, revealing a complexity below the surface. In this below the surface look we might question who we are; it might cause us to pause, or perhaps even motivate us into some sort of action. What is fascinating about his reflection on looking into this water mirror is the understanding of the complexities that can arise upon looking deeply. He echoes a sentiment that what we first see as we look into a mirror might not reveal all; that reflection might not be a surface activity.

Ellington's excerpt brings out the notion that we have multiple identities—in Ellington's case, as a thinker, writer, nixer, player, listener, critic, and corrector. Our students are also thinkers, players, listeners, critics, and so on. We have other identities—gender, religion, and ethnicity. Our students speak one or two or more languages. They have passions that identify them—music, nature, visual art, television, technology, games. Not all of these identities are on the surface, and yet once we come to know our students we find how central their identities can be in how they think, learn, and feel.

The mirror analogies led me to some work of Shirley Brice Heath, specifically her 1999 study with Adelma Roach entitled "Imaginative Actuality: Learning in the Arts during Nonschool Hours." This paper connects the way we look at kids, risk, arts, and practice. Heath compared three types of youth-based organizations—athletic-academic focused, community service centered, and arts-based—over a period of ten years. The arts-based organizations stood out as an arena for students that helped them not only learn art skills, but also to problem solve, express ideas, work collaboratively, articulate strategies, ask and pursue questions, and practice imaginative and creative thinking. She writes:

Young people in arts-based organizations gain *practice* in thinking and talking as adults. They play important roles in their organizations; they have control over centering themselves and working for group excellence in achievement. Their joint

*Patti Christensen, SUAVE arts coach.*

work with adults and peers rides on conversations that test and develop their ideas, explicate processes, and build scenarios of the future. (p. 26) [italics added]

What happens to create the context for such action? Heath argues that risk is an important connection and that risk-taking is fundamental to development. She finds this interesting, especially because these programs are designed to reach children who are at at-risk.

The coaches meetings demand imagination and creation. They serve as a mirror of what is and is not going on in the classroom as well as what is happening in the minds of the coaches. Underlying the coaches meetings is a culture of pondering the possible and improvisation. Coaches meetings often begin with announcements relating to the program (in-service workshops, after-school programs, timesheets for pay, art-related events such as gigs and gallery openings, new commissions), followed by brainstorming and problem solving. The coaches set the agenda by bringing up challenges that usually relate to specific curriculum, such as "I'm in a two-way bilingual second grade classroom, and the teacher wants to teach spelling through the arts. Any suggestions?" or "I'm working with this teacher who just won't plan with me, and when I come in she never has the kids ready. I can't handle it! Help!" The coaches meetings, like the program itself, is not preset, offering plenty of room for experimentation.

The coaches have differing areas of expertise. They include a puppeteer/ storyteller, dancer, poet, musician, mosaic artist, 3-D artist, mime, theater artist, and folk musician. As the group brainstorms, the artists share across disciplines. As a result, they often branch out of their own disciplines when they return to their teachers in the classroom. A visual artist might suggest a poetry activity to a teacher who is focusing on language arts, or a musician might try a dance activity to foster mathematical understanding. This willingness—indeed, interest and enthusiasm—to cross disciplines provides ample opportunity for the coaches to take risks outside of their comfort zone in terms of their art, and in a way provides a model of risk-taking to teachers who are out their realm with many art forms.[1]

My role tends to be lead musician in the ensemble. I control the tune we play (by providing the structure for the meetings) and participate in the brainstorming. Sometimes I bring in new tunes or challenges. For example, one week, a coach brought in a wonderful photograph of young children sitting in a tree. I asked, how could you use this photograph to teach with the arts? This is how one coach reflected on that day:

> Merryl brings in brainstorming—Oh what is this photograph? How can we use this? So it makes us think a lot. But it's playful, fun, because before long we're bouncing ideas off of each other . . . oh it could be used for language arts because it's a picture of a bunch of boys in a tree and we could say, well, what dialogue would go on between these guys, or mathematically, do you see any patterns, or you know they are trunking and branching, that's a kind of pattern. Scientifically, how did this tree get to this size, and getting the children to project, what is the root of this tree, and blah blah blah."

In fact, after this brainstorming activity, a coach brought this particular photograph to a fifth-grade teacher who had expressed interest in photography, and they developed a series of lessons relating to language arts. First, students viewed the photograph and listed things they saw in the photograph and questions they had about it. They shared orally and added to their own lists, if they chose to do so. Next they had a choice: write a letter to someone in the photo; write a letter as if you were someone in the photo; or write a poem relating to the photo (these students were familiar with diamante, haiku, and couplets).[2]

In uncovering the workings of this practicing ensemble, risk emerged over and over as a motivating factor in the coaches' outlook of their role in the classroom and their role as artists. The *American Heritage Dictionary* defines *risk* as "the possibility of suffering harm or loss, danger" (1985, p.1065). Artists in the SUAVE program are drawn to risk, and more often than not they define *risk* as perceiving

---

[1]The teachers of SUAVE have varying degrees of arts backgrounds and experience. It is safe to say, however, that many have not had training in arts education. Arts courses have not been a requirement of many credential programs in the state of California.

[2]This lesson is published in Goldberg, 2001, p. 88.

*The research reported in this chapter was assisted by a joint grant from the John D. and Catherine T. MacArthur Foundation and the Spencer Foundation under the Professional Development Research and Documentation Program. The data presented, the statements made, and the views expressed are solely the responsibility of the authors.*

or exploring the possible. One coach put it this way: "Attempting something beyond the realm of what is known to the person taking the risk." Another said: "that which calls to be . . . a journeyer into the unknown." Shirley Brice Heath writes:

> Risk heightens learning at effective youth-based organizations. While public rhetoric laments the fate of "at-risk youth," our research reveals how youth depend on certain kinds of risk for development. Rather than live at its mercy, youth in arts organizations use the predictability of risks in the arts to intensify the quality of their interactions, products, performances. (Heath & Roach, 1999, p. 27)

Risk-taking within teaching has been identified as a positive and essential ingredient for successful teacher learning and growth (Cohen & Barnes, 1993; Darling-Hammond & McLaughlin, 1996; Fullen, 1995). It requires individuals to engage in uncertain behaviors with a potential for negative consequences (Fullen & Miles, 1992). While risk-taking can evoke feelings of inadequacy and fear of failure, Fullen and Miles (1992) suggest that substantial teacher learning must involve risk-taking. Without uncertainty or difficulty, they claim, change is only "superficial or trivial" (p. 749). Research supports this position, as evidenced by numerous accounts of successful teacher learning involving risk-taking and accompanying emotions of anxiety (see, for example, Ball & Rundquist, 1993; Schifter and Fosnot, 1992; Schweitzer, 1996).

Part of my interest in risk is in uncovering the positive role of risk-taking in teaching and learning, not only for teachers but also for students. Risk-taking is familiar to the coaches; it underlies artistry. Numerous studies indicate that risk-taking is essential to learning, although it is accompanied by anxiety, difficulty, or nervousness. The artist-coaches, however, perceive risk quite differently. "The interaction with the other art coaches, the idea of hiring an artist for the sake of an artist type of a person who is willing to take risks . . . I think that's the luckiest place to be an artist." The artists have described risk as

- Trying something new without certainty of the results
- Attempting something beyond the realm of what is known to the person taking the risk
- revealing, igniting, shaping, knowing, kindling
- that which calls to be, to be accomplished, and seems beyond; usually connected with fear and failing, or exhilaration to jump and dive in and try

When asked about their definition of themselves as artists, it was no surprise that risk also defined their views of themselves as artists. For example, an artist is

- One who takes risks in society to speak their truth through the mediums of dance, visual arts, performance, and poetry
- One who ardently "arts," a way of being, seeing, hearing, using all the senses to perceive dreams and realities

- Someone who takes risks at making people feel and see our own lives
- A creator, transformer, innovator, interpreter; person who colors life, who redefines and recreates reality, who crosses established boundaries, who speaks universal languages, and who reaches the soul

Rather than focus on prevention and detention for at-risk youth, the organizations Heath examined urge creativity and invention with young people as "competent risk-takers across a range of media and situations" (Heath & Roach, 1999, p. 21). She continues,

> The high risk embedded in the performances and exhibitions of these organizations creates an atmosphere in which students know how to solicit support, challenge themselves and others, and share work and resources whenever possible. Critique, as an *improvisational* and reciprocal process, amplifies *practice* gained during project planning. (p. 26) [italics added]

In the workings and function of the SUAVE coaches meetings, improvisation abounds. The coaches thrive on it. As the jam sessions evolve, the layers of complexity and vagueness become even thicker. Ideas are played out, transformed, and then replayed. The initial look into the mirror that begins all practice sessions turns from the surface to misty. Misty leads to uncertainty, creating the space for risk-taking. This is where the magic begins, and uncertainty can lead to the possible or to defeat.

For people who are not artists or involved in the artistic process, the vagueness and uncertainty might be uncomfortable. For the coaches, it is a way of living. I also believe it is a natural way of being for children as they embark on learning. Children are natural risk-takers—parents know this from experience, especially parents of toddlers! Children learn through exploring and trying new activities, by taking risks.

## Practice as Risk-Taking

The coaches' practice sessions set the stage for risk-taking both professionally and personally. The coaches are accustomed to taking risks, or exploration as artists. Surely there is some spillover into their role as professional developers. As well, they are not afraid of failure or mistakes. Partly this can be attributed to their lives as artists where paying attention to "failure" and mistakes can provide opportunity. Some of the most important discoveries made by individuals stem from mistakes. Artists thrive on what others might call mistakes. The mistakes often give birth to wonderful and new ideas. Artists often encourage the use of mistakes as potential sources of imagination and learning.

The weekly coaches meetings create a culture that builds trust, confidence, security, support, and ownership, and offers an opportunity to practice flexibility and experience modeling. These elements emerge from the constant improvisations and reflections shared among the participants.

**Trust and confidence:** Trust is built through sustained improvisation and jamming in the form of sharing and brainstorming together. The atmosphere doesn't promote competition because the artists are from different disciplines.

> According to one coach, " Merryl's made this clear. Hey if it doesn't work, you know, we really emphasize the process, so if it doesn't come out picture-perfect then we know we can try it again. So it's a very organic way of working, and it gives you a lot of confidence." Another coach put it this way, "[I feel] more confident in myself to try new ideas. You know we often talk about risk-taking and I realize I'm this risk-taker. I'll do many, many things for the first time myself with a teacher and the teacher may not know it until after we do it because deep down inside I'm wondering, Okay, is this going to work out? But definitely more confident; more confident to try those other areas like music and drama." An interviewer followed up, "What helped you be more confident?" The art coach replied, "the arts coach meetings are just terrific and the in-services very supportive; building trust between that relationship with your teacher, and if I had a question that maybe a teacher might ask me, then I could say openly, 'well I think so and so knows more about that . . . ' I'll ask her at our next brainstorming meeting."

**Security and support:** The coaches will say that the SUAVE "gig" is not for the money, although the steady income provides security. Almost none of the coaches had health insurance prior to SUAVE, and many are in their late thirties to late fifties. Feeling secure has enabled a number of them to focus on their own art and even apply for new commissions, create new performances, or begin new musical groups.

> "We're all experiencing the same or similar things. There's a lot of support." "Everyone is very supportive; you really feel like you're not doing it alone; you're not, and you can bring these things there and there's a cushion."

Support comes in the form of sharing beliefs and techniques, as well as talking through how to work with challenging teachers and subject matter. Coaches also find support among the group in terms of their own artistry, sharing their work, ideas, and materials with each other.

**Ownership:** "The coaches meetings have been real helpful camaraderie, yeah just the opening up of 'where we can go where can we take this?' I mean it's kind of like we have a little ownership in the program because we find out that we need this, so pretty soon we get this."

**Flexibility:** Things constantly change in SUAVE, for there is not a pre-fixed curriculum, or set of must-do activities to share with teachers. A culture of invention is valued. "What I love about SUAVE is that I'm constantly learning, and the art coach meetings that occur on Tuesdays, I just really need that, because of bouncing ideas off of each other."

**Modeling:** What goes on in coaches meetings in terms of the process of brainstorming is often taken into the work with the teachers. Interviewer: "You learn the process and you go out and you do the same kind of thing?" Coach: "Yes."

In addition to setting the stage for risk-taking, certain philosophical tenets and practices emerge.

- Basic beliefs about art and arts in education are reinforced. "Art is really basic, and this is validated through the coaches meetings."
- Attention to what is possible drives the philosophy of the coaches. "Through this job I'm in contact with teachers and coaches and can see how that brings that much variety, different ways of doing things, and different processes. It has made me more of a believer in the creative process, more than I was already."
- A culture of invention is created, valued, and reinforced. "It is nice to know we don't have limitations; we didn't have a set way to go; we could just try it and see how it felt, and it was just real organic in the process and nothing was a mistake. I mean all of that made it real easy to try things and push yourself where you think you couldn't get pushed."
- Coaches are motivated to exhibit and/or perform. "[The coaches meetings] have inspired me to try new things, but also to do it more as an artist. I think it's gotten me kind of motivated to do more or branch out in different directions."

## Coaching and Classroom Activity

When the artist-coaches gather weekly to practice or jam, the improvisations take the form of sharing and learning techniques, assessing strategies with particular teachers, brainstorming activities, and learning art forms from each other. The artists often become animated as they share ideas from their own art forms and build upon them as they hear ideas from other art forms. For example, in considering the challenge of introducing study of the planets, a dancer suggests moving the kids as if they were the planets. A musician suggests a sound piece based on the length of time it takes for the planets to move around the sun; a visual artists suggests creating a mobile; and the drama specialist suggests creating a production involving backdrops and integrating the ideas of the others. When the activities are shared with various teachers in their classrooms, the coaches have many suggestions and ideas. The resulting classroom activities often involve areas out of the expertise of the coach, but they show an eagerness to try. The artists, as professional developers, expand their repertoire in terms of art forms, activities, and techniques to suggest to teachers.

Often, issues related to English language learners will emerge. This is especially true for the bilingual coaches, many of whom can empathize with the children. Sometimes the issues raised are positive, and sometimes they have to do with needs of ELL students that are not being addressed. In these cases, the coaches do all within their power to bring forth ways to better serve English language learners or to directly work with some children to ensure their participation. The lessons brought forward at coaches meetings serve to inform all the coaches and no doubt have an impact on their practices as well.

The artists also use the coaches meetings to brainstorm strategies for working with teachers. Each coach works with ten to twenty, teachers, all with differing levels of arts background and all with individual classroom agendas. It is not unusual for a coach to be baffled about how to reach a certain teacher or frustrated with a teacher with whom there is a personality clash. When coaches are having difficulties or challenges with teachers, the group works together to brainstorm ways to improve the situation. The coaches also commiserate with each other; each one has needed help at the coaches meetings. Often, in fact, situations from the past become "case studies" as the group deliberates on a current situation.

Fortunately for SUAVE, all the case studies involving challenging situations have ended in success. Where it seemed as if the teachers would never overcome their resistance, it has turned out that not only did the teachers overcome their resistance, but that they have become strong supporters of the role of art in learning and in living. Knowing this—having a SUAVE coach history—enables the group to embrace resistance and challenges with a hopeful outlook. An atmosphere that supports a philosophy that change in a teacher's practice might seem small but is really a big step for the teacher is key.

## Coaching and Artistic Expansion

The coaches often discuss expanding their own personal areas of art. In the realm of personal development, the artists reveal a sense of freedom from coaching meetings that spills over to their own art making. This is probably due to a number of factors. The coaching job gives them financial security to take on creative endeavors that they might not otherwise feel they have the time for. One coach recently won a huge public commission for giant mosaic and iron structures in Pacific Beach, California. She said she felt that she could apply for the project because of the security of SUAVE and her motivation to create artwork related to the theme of the beach. The coaches are motivated by their interdisciplinary discussions. Some have begun collaborations with each other, pushing them into new artistic realms. One coach, a performer, has become interested in directing as a result of organizing classroom activities and in-service workshops.

## Impact of Practice

It is clear that the coaching meetings are meaningful and even make a difference in the lives of the artists, both as professional developers in elementary classrooms and in their own areas of art. The program improves as the artists share across disciplines and experiment with different art forms with their teacher partners. Teachers, knowing that the coaches meet every week, have also become accustomed to asking coaches to ask other coaches for advice.

The coaches meetings are in part the glue that keeps the program successful and the artists (the professional developers) not only interested but also continually acting as learners and risk-takers. The program and the professional developers are not static; it is a dynamic culture. Mistakes are looked upon as opportunities by the artists themselves and by the program as a whole. As in all practice sessions, there is attention to getting the notes right, which in our case is the concept of finding ways to reach teachers as learners; and there is improvisation, where the real magic happens.

## Summary

Practicing and improvising every week for two hours is critical for the professional developers of SUAVE as well for the success and dynamic nature of the overall program. Any meeting would probably be beneficial. The structure of our coaching meetings, like a good practice or jam session, involves the coaches in mindful activity. The improvisations or brainstorming set the stage for creative and reflective activity and encourage risk-taking, a crucial element in transformation and learning. The fact that competition is not a factor at these meetings in all likelihood benefits the process. The leadership engages in brainstorming with the group and often acts as a timekeeper, or brings the group back on track if there has been a long tangent. This role seems to benefit the overall process.

The sustained nature of the meetings creates a history that makes "case studies" available. The coaches refer back to similar situations, often with hindsight and a sense of humor. The camaraderie created through these meetings bonds the coaches in significant ways. Some have begun to collaborate with each other both in the context of the program as well as in their own artwork. Their beliefs about arts in education as well as the artistic process have been reinforced or strengthened; a culture of invention is created, and limitations are set aside; the possible is valued; and the coaches are motivated both within the program and in their own disciplines.

Practice, risks, thinking outside the box, thinking creatively and critically, reflecting, concentrating, listening, responding, reacting—all are elements of the ongoing mix. Like Duke Ellington's look into the pool, the mirrors cause more and more reflections, adding vagueness to the process. In that vagueness, complexity emerges as innovators begin to look at shapes and transform them, redefine them, and recreate them. Reality, as one coach said, is redefined and recreated. Risk-taking becomes play. Play becomes practice. Practice begets the possible. The artists play with the possible both in the jam sessions and on their own as they bring their improvisations back to the classroom, all the while embracing the vague and misty overtones. They are not afraid of defeat. The program ripples.

## *References*

*American Heritage Dictionary,* Second College Edition (1985). Boston: Houghton Mifflin Company.

Ball, D. L., & Rundquist, S. S. (1993). Collaboration as a context for joining teacher learning with learning about teaching. In D. K. Cohen, M. W. McLaughlin, & J. E. Talbert (Eds.), *Teaching for understanding: Challenges for policy and practice* (pp. 13–42). San Francisco: Jossey-Bass.

Cohen, D. K., & Barnes, C. A. (1993). Conclusion: A new pedagogy for policy. In D. K. Cohen, M. W. McLaughlin, & J. E. Talbert (Eds.), *Teaching for understanding: Challenges for policy and practice* (pp. 240–275). San Francisco: Jossey-Bass.

Darling-Hammond, L., & McLaughlin, M. W. (1996). Policies that support professional development in an era of reform. In M. W. McLaughlin & I. Oberman (Eds.), *Teacher learning: New policies, new practices* (pp. 202–218). New York: Teachers College Press.

Ellington, D. (1973). *Music is my mistress.* New York: Da Capo Press.

Fullan, M. G. (1995). The limits and the potential of professional development. In T. R. Guskey & M. Huberman (Eds.), *Professional development in education: New paradigms and practices.* New York: Teachers College Press.

Fullan, M. G., & Miles, M. B. (1992). Getting reform right: What works and what doesn't. *Phi Delta Kappan,* 7 (10), 744–752.

Goldberg, M. (1997). *Arts and learning: An integrated approach to teaching and learning in multicultural and multilingual settings.* New York: Longman.

Goldberg, M. (2001). *Arts and learning: An integrated approach to teaching and learning in multicultural and multilingual settings,* 2nd ed. New York: Longman.

Goldberg, M., & Bossenmeyer, M. (1998). Shifting the role of arts in education. *Principal* 77 (4), 56–58.

Gottlieb, R. (Ed.) (1996). *Reading jazz: A gathering of autobiography, reportage, and criticism from 1919 to now.* New York: Pantheon Books.

Heath, Shirley Brice, with Adelma Roach. (1999). Imaginative actuality: Learning in the arts during nonschool hours. In *Champions of change: The impact of learning on the arts.* The President's Committee on the Arts and Humanities.

Howard, V. A. (1991). And practice drives me mad; or, the drudgery of drill. *Harvard Educational Review,* 61 (1), 80–87.

Schifter, D., & Fosnot, C. T. (1992). *Reconstructing mathematics education: Stories of teachers meeting the challenge of reform.* New York: Teachers College Press.

Schweitzer, K. (1996). The search for the perfect resource. In D. Schifter (Ed.), *What's happening in math class? Reconstructing professional identities,* Vol. 2 (pp. 46–65). New York: Teachers College Press.

# 11

## Artists in the Classroom: The Role of Resistance in Positive Change

**Merryl Goldberg, Tom Bennett, and Victoria Jacobs**

*This is a process. And I'm really—the kids are getting the process—and I'm getting a philosophy of art. And so I kind of chilled out and thought about it and [I realized] I'm not going to get this [water color painting] step by step. I am going to get more of a philosophy in the process.*

Lani, fourth-grade teacher

### KEY CONCEPTS

- Process
- Resistance
- Tension
- Transformation
- Beliefs and action
- Art technique versus the artistic process
- Who is an artist?

This chapter tells the story of a fourth-grade teacher's learning about the arts and learning to teach through the arts. It is about the teacher's relationships with two very different artists. It is a story replete with tension, resistance, and epiphany. It takes place over a three-year period. And it has a happy ending.

## Context

Transformation of teaching beliefs and actions is often the goal of professional development programs. A question for professional development rests in ways to promote and encourage shifts in beliefs and subsequent practices. This chapter looks at how the coaching relationship causes changes of belief and practice by highlighting one teacher's profound changes over a period of time. Most teacher-artist relationships in SUAVE are overwhelmingly positive. The relationship that is the focus of this chapter, however, was arguably the worst, at least on the surface. It was tenuous both personally and professionally. But, the surface appearance hid something quite different.

Increasingly, learning through the arts is becoming a component of arts education and an issue in terms of the role arts play in a balanced curriculum (ASCD Curriculum Update, 1998). According to CDE Arts Work: Task Force on Arts Education (1997), "improving literacy in other subjects through ways of knowing provided by the arts" is an essential role of arts in the classroom. Learning through the arts does not diminish the importance of learning about the arts. Rather, it expands the role of arts in the education of all children. In addition to educating students about arts as disciplines (ideally, from arts educators), classroom teachers are being asked to integrate the arts as a strategy to accommodate the variety of ways in which children learn. Most classroom teachers, however, are not trained to teach about the arts or to utilize the arts as a teaching strategy.

It is not unusual to find artists in schools as artists-in-residence or doing special projects. Research has highlighted teacher-artist partnerships in which teachers have learned about the arts from professional artists (Upitis, Soren, & Smithrim, 1998). This chapter takes a different perspective. It looks closely at relationships between teachers and artists focused on breaking down the barriers that separate disciplines as well as learning about the arts in and of themselves. At the same time, it responds to a larger issue in the professional development of teachers, that of isolation. According to Mike Rose (1995), a challenge to professional development is breaking down the isolation of teachers and honoring their experience as a starting point. Researchers have argued that ideal professional development offers participants meaningful engagement with ideas, is responsive to teachers' needs, is linked to teacher contexts, and involves teachers in designing their own learning experiences (Little, 1993; Darling-Hammond & McLaughlin, 1996; Lewis, 1998). "Professional development is currently limited," argues Michael Fullen (1995, p. 258), "because it is seen as and experienced as separated events, as though teachers' learning can be segmented from their regular work." SUAVE seeks to bridge the gap between teacher learning and classroom practice through "on-the job" (in-class) coaching.

*Eduardo Parra, arts coach.*

The coach's role is multifold and customized to each teacher's needs. Depending on the learning style and needs of each teacher, the coach can act in many ways. We have found that there is no single recipe for success. The coach can be a resource, a role model, a support person, a motivator, or a person to bounce ideas off of; someone who provides feedback, inspiration, encouragement, temptation, guidance, assistance, ideas, or a safe environment for risk-taking. The coach also can provide answers to questions in context and share technical expertise as well as a passion for arts and for learning.

To illustrate a transformation through coaching, this chapter will take a case study approach. Lani is a fourth-grade teacher, and her coach is Fernando.[1] Out of the ten teacher-artist pairs at this school, they had the most strained coaching relationship, but profound changes resulted. The events begin in September of year 1, when Lani began work with her first coach, Karen, and continue in September of year 2, when Lani began work with her second coach, Fernando.

Individualized coaching of teachers by artists has been quite successful even under the most strained conditions. Yet, when we looked at a particularly strained relationship, we find that the teacher transformation blossomed in four areas.

1. The teacher's notion or definition of who an artist is expands.
2. The teacher's understanding of the artistic process is broadened from viewing art as the acquisition of a set of techniques and skills to incorporating the role of experimenting as an important aspect of the artistic process.
3. The teacher relates and applies the artistic process to academic learning by comparing the importance of experimenting to understanding concepts.

---

[1]The names of the teachers and coaches have been changed.

4. The teacher develops personally in the area of arts appreciation both in her reflections and in her awareness of her students' knowledge of the arts.

Though the majority of classrooms teachers, coaches, and observers described coaching relationships positively, what became increasingly evident was that, in the few classrooms with clear tensions between the coach and the teacher, many important things were still happening. In fact, even in the most strained relationships, the teacher and the students underwent profound changes and learning. Six changes have been found in all classrooms, regardless of the quality of the teacher-coach relationship:

1. Teachers (and other students) see students in new ways.
2. Teachers reach more students, and more students get to "shine."
3. Students get excited about learning (art or other content).
4. Students are exposed to the arts.
5. Students are motivated and involved in learning.
6. Students (and often the teacher) are involved in some risk-taking.

Most of these have to do with student learning. Teachers have also made profound changes in their beliefs and actions after the coach has left. This brings us back to Lani and Fernando. During coaching, it appeared as if Lani was not learning and was merely tolerating Fernando as her weekly coach. What unfolded, however, is a story of profound change out of tension and resistance.

In a best situation, the coach, teacher, and students are learners, are risk-takers, are enthusiastic, gain confidence, are involved, value and respect each other, value the communication of skills and the sharing of ideas. The arts become tangible, as does learning in the content areas. In coaching partnerships in which tension or resistance is a factor, by contrast, coaches, teachers, or both do not feel valued or respected. Their interpretations of the coach's role differ, as do their teaching philosophies and/or organizational or teaching styles. Their interpersonal skills (listening, expressing ideas) are poor or mismatched. Other struggles might be related to power struggles, gender issues, or cultural issues. In the following chart, it is fascinating and perplexing to note that despite the working and personal relationships, positive changes occurred in all pairs.

| Personal relationship | Professional relationship | Teacher learning as evidenced in beliefs | Teacher learning as evidenced in actions |
|---|---|---|---|
| Good | Good | Positive changes | Positive changes |
| Tenuous | Resistant | Positive changes | Positive changes |

The surprise, of course, is that tenuous personal and resistant professional relationships can result in positive teacher learning. What, then, is the cause of such resistance, and how can that resistance lead to a positive experience?

Lani, a fourth-grade teacher, teaches in a two-way bilingual situation. In the two-way bilingual program, all students learn English and all students learn Spanish. Lani, who teaches in English, is teamed with Andrea, who teaches in Spanish. The students see each teacher for one-half of their classes. Lani and Andrea, along with eight other teachers in their school, all receive an hour of individualized coaching each week from Fernando.

## The Story Begins

Lani is in her second year of coaching. Last year Karen, a visual artist, was her coach. Karen is classically trained as a visual and mosaic artist and has a degree in art history from an American university. The two got along gloriously. This year, Lani has been working with Fernando, an all-around "talented" (her word) artist with expertise in drama, music, and visual arts. Fernando, a native of Mexico, was not formally trained in the arts. Compared to Karen, who could be considered a "trained" artist, Fernando could be categorized as a "folk" artist. As the story unfolds, we see how this distinction plays itself out in relationship to Lani's understanding of the nature of the artistic process as well as the role of art in teaching and learning.

Lani and Fernando's relationship, from the perspectives of Lani, Fernando, and an outside observer, is tenuous at best. At times it could be described as painful. Their interactions are cautious, and neither is happy with the relationship. Communication, listening, and growing together are very important to Lani. Midway through her year of working with Fernando, she defines a successful teacher-coach relationship:

> I would define [success in a teacher-coach relationship] as a lot of giving and taking, and a lot of sharing together and growing together, and just a lot, lots of communication; lots of listening, which is part of communication, and lots of building, kind of like building blocks. I was kind of thinking that my last year's relationship . . . I saw it more; I saw those building blocks and that growth, and that building.

Lani has expectations of her coach. She expects him to lead her. She wants to be shown techniques and skills. She relates her definition to a typical coaching situation as in sports.

In gathering definitions from the broader group of SUAVE teachers and coaches, we find that the coach is not defined like a typical soccer or football coach, where there is a hierarchical power relationship. Instead, the relationship is a professional-professional model, meaning that both the artist and the teacher have expertise, and the intersection of their expertise can create incredible opportunities for children (indeed for all partners). The teacher has expertise in curriculum and pedagogy, how children learn, and the specific needs of her students. The artist has expertise in an art discipline and in the process of art and arts integration, and has a passion for arts as a language. Together, they form a powerful team.

Lani not only had a different view of the coach's role, but different expectations. The differing expectations created tension.

> With a coach I would have *expectations* of leading me, because the end goal that I would see is next year leaving me where I can take and do on my own, so my expectations were that the coaches [would] give me things and let me watch and help me train and do all these things. You know, and have me participate and you know, we can build from together, but that I can be left on my own and take it from there . . . because *now* the coach has the expertise . . . expertise in the arts, that's why they're the coach. It would be like, you know, in sports, like where I see my son, like soccer, you know, it's teaching the little *skill* and then I can go from there.

Lani prefers not to be surprised. Conflict between Lani and Fernando occurs when she is surprised by what happens during a coaching session. The surprise often related to Fernando's letting the students "experiment." Talking about planning and what goes on in the classroom during coaching, she says:

> It's still a surprise to me . . . So, it's like I can't interact because I'm not sure what's going on or where it's leading or what's happening. [He's indirect] and sometimes I get this feeling that Fernando doesn't want, doesn't like me to interrupt or talk, or interact. . . . I kind of got these vibes like he was annoyed.

Lani reveals that she has changed her expectations of their working relationship and what she might expect to learn from Fernando. She discusses her expectations in terms of how she thinks students learn, which is that they need something "concrete."

> And, I guess I lowered my expectations . . . in terms of what I'm going to get out of it and what I expect. . . . If I don't come up with the things myself and do the lessons and you know be really specific, the kids aren't going to learn . . . the concrete. And it's hard to take and make it concrete and understandable for the kids. I want someone—a self-starter. . . . Because we don't know much, you know, with the arts. . . . so anything that he teaches, we're going to, like eat up. So, any little *technique* or something that he gives us, we're going to love it, because that's what we're here for.

Lani explains what she means by "self-starter" by comparing Fernando to Karen, her coach the previous year. Her expectations of the coach are evident: She expects the coach to take the lead. Her understanding of an artist is also clear: An artist has formal training and background knowledge in the discipline. This definition fits Karen quite well. But, it doesn't fit Fernando. This played itself out both years. When Lani decided that she wanted to introduce Western artists and musicians to her students, she focused on visual artists, including Georgia O'Keefe, when Karen was her coach. With Fernando, she wanted to introduce Beethoven and other well-known composers.

> [Karen and I were] such such opposites, but we both grew; we'd laugh at it, you know, because like Georgia O'Keefe; I was like, we want to do the artist Georgia O'Keefe and I can tell the life story but I want you to do the art with it. So I told the art, the life, and that's all I wanted to do. Beethoven [with Fernando], I said I'll tell them their life stories; you just do the music. So Georgia O'Keefe, she says, 'Oh, we'll have them do water colors'; she says, 'You know, could bring in . . . flowers. So I bring in these plastic flowers and Karen brings in all these supplies and she looks at these and she's like, 'Lani, these are plastic.' Yeah, well . . . and she's like, 'No they can't, you know, draw from plastic!' I said, 'Well, why not?' [Discussion of drawing from science] and she kept *pulling me*. . . . she gave me the courage to try new things.

Lani is concerned that the coaching time is not useful and, in fact, is "cutting into my instruction time."

> He comes out here and he entertains, and that's fine, but after an hour a week of him entertaining is not—I feel like it's cutting into my instruction time; the kids aren't getting anything; the kids aren't able to get things, but he does that because he likes doing it. And, I'm not a part of that; we're all watching the Fernando act. I think he wants to please us instead of just doing his thing and going with his talent.

Lani begins to consider her role in the relationship:

> You know, it could be my mistake too, because I was used to—I want him to take the lead and I want to learn from it; but this is not working. I'm just going to have to take—I feel like I have a student teacher in the room.

Lani struggles with wanting concrete techniques, skills, and ideas from her coach. Her notion of art is that it is a set of specific techniques and skills that one acquires. In terms of application to the classroom, she wants to learn these techniques and skills and how to apply them in such a way that she sees results in the form of tangible products. She is uncomfortable with surprises and is very conscious of when she believes time is being wasted. As the year goes on, however, Lani begins to reconsider the role of art and also the role of the artist-coach in her classroom.

## The Story Continues: The End of the Year Is upon Us, and Teachers Reflect on What They Have Learned

Lani reflects on the year in a focus group interview with other teachers from her school. They come to a number of realizations about themselves as teachers, their expectations, and art. The teachers begin by describing the way in which Fernando worked in their classrooms.

> *Lani:*  He enjoys exploratory—that's his love rather than task-oriented. But as teachers, we're so task-oriented. Karen was a little more task-oriented too with us at least. And Fernando's a big change. Karen would follow the flow of us a bit more.
>
> *Andrea:*  She [Karen] would do an art lesson and we would finish up and then the next week there was different lesson. So we were used to seeing a final product and it was done fast. With Fernando it was like we were going on forever! But now that I look back, I think it wouldn't take us any shorter next year because now we know all the preparation time it takes to make the children feel comfortable.
>
> *Lani:*  Teachers are A type personalities! Then we have Fernando drop into our room—it was like someone from outer space! I wonder if he sees teachers are different from artists—our perspective.

A little later in the conversation, Lani reaches a critical turning point. She articulates her understanding that art is a process in addition to a set of techniques and skills (which she calls a "discipline").

> I didn't mind teaching art, but I used to see art more as a discipline. We'll teach Georgia O'Keefe, and then I'd give a test—and Karen used to make fun of me for giving a test. But I had to give a test on everything I taught—and now I see it as more of being involved and more that the kids become it and learn it more. It's okay to experiment. I do more art more now as experimentation and not as a canned lesson.

## The End of the Coaching

At the end of year, Lani reflects on her last two years of coaching. Here we see an amazing turning point in Lani's conception of art and its use in the classroom. She articulates art as a process as well as a set of techniques and skills. She also recognizes how important that process is to students as they grapple with understanding of concepts. She even goes so far as to apply the idea of experimenting (which she now sees as a defining aspect of art) to other subject areas, such as mathematics.

This is a process. And I'm really—the kids are getting the process—and I'm getting a philosophy of art. And so I kind of chilled out and thought about it and [I realized] I'm not going to get this [water color painting] step by step. I am going to get more of a philosophy in the process. . . . I thought, it's neat with the two years. With [the first coach] I really did learn a lot of techniques, and I really did learn a lot of things I could teach the kids, and with Fernando, I did learn a different philosophy, which is good. So I learned two major things. So each year I really learned something. *So even though I felt like this year I wasn't, I was and I did.*

Lani continues to describe her changing and broader view of artists. She accepts that artists can be formally or informally trained, and that both are acceptable.

He would come in and I learned that it was all right to spend time, what's the word, not practicing—experimenting. The experimenting is the process, a process of art, and it's okay. It's okay to have the kids experiment and it's okay for the kids to watch him perform. You know, I felt frustrated that he did that a lot. . . . But you know what? That was good for the kids to see and then we got into where they were actually doing it themselves. The technique and all that's good, but it's okay to just get some crayons, a pencil and paper, and just let them do—and they don't need to know—I mean I think it's still important to know the great musicians and different types of music. . . . *But it's okay just to do without having any knowledge. It's okay. That's okay; I've changed my thought.*

Here we find Lani reflecting upon how important the artistic process is for her students. We see her ease up on the element of time and control in learning. We also see her relate artistic processes to learning in the academic areas.

You know, I'm so into time frames in that we have to get this and this covered, but I also now feel that the experimenting process is necessary and even when it comes to math now, I have my kids experiment; I don't get as uptight. So, I've brought it over to other areas. . . . Maybe if Fernando was here last year I wouldn't have, but it was good to have Karen first. This is my third year of teaching, so I think it takes that long to give up control. So maybe I was ready to give up some control. And he's helped me. I had to; I had no choice with him (laughter) no choice. I feel confident that it does help the children learn, so it's not just a waste of time; it's not just doing arts and crafts. It's beneficial to the academic learning. So I really feel it's not like on a Friday afternoon when you have nothing to do, it's okay to do art. It's okay to do all the time because, it's you know, as long as it goes with the program, the kids are learning.

## The Year Following Coaching

A test of learning and change is whether and how it is sustained. Seven months after the end of her two years of coaching, there are profound changes in Lani's philosophy and practice.

> [One of the things] I've learned is to give more control to the kids . . . I think my teaching style because of SUAVE has changed a little bit and [the students] see that, so I think they know they have an opportunity. . . . I'm the facilitator and not the teacher. . . . And one of the things is not to be as rigid when it comes to art. And, all subjects actually, because it kind of filters in. But also with that, let them [the students] become the creative person. . . . For me, that's a really big step. It really is. . . . Because you know you see how it works. It's not chaos. You know I don't like chaos.

In observing her, we see not only transformed teaching techniques, but also development in recognizing the kids' attention to the music and complimenting them on that!

> The good thing that surprised me when we did the Mexican hat dance was how they were listening to the rhythm of the music to do the dance. I was really surprised by that; pleasantly surprised, how they corrected themselves without me even having to say anything.

On integrating the arts this year (as compared to the last two years), she says she thinks she's even doing more.

## Lessons of Resistance

A number of lessons can be drawn from this happy ending. First and foremost, resistance can be a positive factor in creating meaningful changes in beliefs and practice. This is as true for Lani and other teachers as for children. Breaking out from the social practices that are dominant in our cultures might be fundamental to meaningful change, which underscores the importance of paying attention to the positive role of resistance. For example, resisting arbitrary authority and taking control of one's own learning might enable teaching hope (Kohl, 1994). Lani's resistance ultimately led to a number of changes both in belief and practice. Resistance is the outcome underscoring a belief system that is being challenged. The challenging of beliefs can be key in growth and change.

As a result of being challenged throughout an entire year, Lani comes to understand that artists can be formally or informally trained. Prior to coaching, she had a narrow definition of an artist, based on a traditional view of a classically trained artist. Thus, her notion and definition of an artist has been greatly broadened. This realization led to other changes.

1. Lani's conception of art and the artistic process has broadened from a view that focused on art as technique, skill, and product to that of a process involving experimentation as well as technique and skill that may or may not result in a product.
2. Lani comes to understand how the artistic process is important to academic learning as well as being important onto itself. She applies this concept to other areas. "It is important to experiment in math."
3. On her own, Lani has developed personally in the area of the arts. She recognizes the music and artistic understanding of her students as they dance the Mexican hat dance. She has shown growth in the arts as a discipline.

So what has enable Lani to make these changes in her thinking and action? What is the relationship of tension and resistance to teacher learning? What led Lani to question her beliefs and to move toward changing them? Could Lani have changed her beliefs in a shorter time frame?

One thing that is a constant is that the coach keeps coming back. Lani is confronted with Fernando on a weekly basis for a year, and she realizes that she needs to do something to make their weekly work together feel grounded. She sees the good influence the coach and the arts have on her students despite their relationship. The *sustained* nature of the relationship no doubt is influential in the ability to change.

Lani is receiving individualized coaching, but it is within the context of a community of teacher learners at her school. Nine other teachers have the same coach. In the May group interview, we see power in the community, and it manifests itself in the reflective thinking that evolves. The role of *community* and a community that reflects on practice could be factors. Furthermore, the coaching is *customized*, not a predetermined set of techniques or objectives that the teacher must achieve. Although this was a source of tension because it resulted in "surprises" for Lani (which she didn't like), the customizing also forced Lani and Fernando to persist in finding ways to work with one another.

Finally, a differing point of view about the role of the coach or differing expectations of a coach can cause tension and resistance. This played itself out over and over throughout Lani's work with Fernando.

## Conclusions

Whether we are students or teachers, learning can be time-consuming, perhaps even frustrating. This is especially true when there are barriers in terms of cultural expectations and understandings, including understandings of the role of arts and who an artist is. Lani and Fernando had vastly different notions of an artist. At first, Lani is more willing to work with an artist who is trained according to

Western standards. Fernando presents an interesting dilemma because he is not what she thinks of as an artist.

In some ways, ELL students may not present themselves according to teachers' notions of students. Understanding and working with them requires a willingness to learn about them, not to simply teach them. Changes like Lani's are profound. She realized that the artistic process she somewhat begrudgingly learned from Fernando was not at all antithetical to the process of learning that in her heart she knew was important to her students. To her credit, not only did she learn a great deal, but her learning had a lasting impact on her teaching even years later.

## *References*

ASCD Curriculum Update. (1998). *Arts education: A cornerstone of basic education.* Alexandria, VA: Association for Supervision and Curriculum Development.

CDE Arts Work: Task Force on Arts Education. (1997). Current developments in arts education. California Department of Education.

Darling-Hammond, L., & McLaughlin, M. W. (1996). Policies that support professional development in an era of reform. In M. W. McLaughlin & I. Oberman (Eds.), *Teacher learning: New policies new practice.* New York: Teachers College Press.

Fullen, M. (1995). The limits and the potential of professional development. In T. R. Guskey & M. Huberman (Eds.), *Professional development in education: New paradigms and practices.* New York: Teachers College Press.

Goldberg, M. (1997). *Arts and learning: An integrated approach to teaching and learning in multicultural and multilingual settings.* New York: Longman.

Goldberg, M. R., & Bossenmeyer, M. (1998). Shifting the role of arts in education. *Principal, 77* (4), 56–58.

Kohl, H. (1994). *I won't learn from you and other thoughts on creative maladjustment.* New York: The New Press.

Lewis, A. (1998). A new consensus emerges on the characteristics of good professional development. In R. Tovey (Ed.), *Professional development.* Harvard Education Letter Focus Series No. 4, 1–3.

Little, J. W. (1993). Teachers' professional development in a climate of educational reform. *Educational Evaluation and Analysis, 15* (2), 129–151.

Rose, M. (1995). *Possible lives: The promise of public education in America.* New York: Penguin.

Smylie, M. A. (1995). Teacher learning in the workplace: Implications for school reform. In T. R. Guskey & M. Huberman (Eds.), *Professional development in education: New paradigms and practices.* New York: Teachers College Press.

Upitis, R., Soren, B. J., & Smithrim, K. (1998). Teacher transformation through the arts. Paper presented at the annual meeting of the American Educational Research Association (AERA), April 13–17, San Diego, CA.

# Biographies

**Tom Bennett** is an associate professor of mathematics education at California State University San Marcos. His research interests include how children develop an understanding of mathematics, international issues in mathematics education, and how the arts can help students develop an understanding of core content.

**Eduardo García** teaches Latin American music at California State University in San Marcos where he directs the Andean Ensemble. He also works in SUAVE. He has performed both as a classical guitarist and with Latin American music ensembles in the United States and Mexico. Lately he has been playing with words when the muses fly in the vicinity.

**Merryl Goldberg** is a professor of visual and performing arts at California State University San Marcos, where she teaches courses on arts and learning, and music. She is a professional saxophonist and recording artist, having toured internationally for thirteen years with the Klezmer Conservatory Band. Her publications include *Arts and Learning: An Integrated Approach to Teaching and Learning in Multicultural and Multilingual Settings* (Longman) and *Arts as Education* (Harvard Educational Review), as well as several articles on learning through the arts. She is the recipient of Spencer, John D. and Catherine T. MacArthur, and Fulbright-Hays Foundations grants relating to her work with arts in the schools.

**Leah Goodwin,** president and chief operating officer for VSA arts of California (formerly Very Special Arts California), has over a decade of arts management and development experience. Her specific focus has been developing and expanding arts education programs in the areas of curriculum development, arts integration, cultural sensitivity, and accessibility. Most notably, as director of education and access at the California Center for the Arts, Escondido, she spent six years creating what is now a statewide model visual and performing art education program. Goodwin, a Huntington Beach resident, was born and raised in Berkeley, California. She is a published poet and a Fullbright scholarship recipient.

**Victoria Jacobs** is an associate professor of mathematics education at San Diego State University. She received her doctorate in educational psychology in 1996 from the University of Wisconsin-Madison. Her research interests focus on understanding and promoting the professional development of teachers. She designs, directs, and studies professional development opportunities that involve long-term collaborations with teachers and school districts. She is also interested in investigating children's mathematical thinking, and research in this area provides the foundation for most of her professional development work with teachers.

**Sherry Reid** is a first-grade teacher at Valley Center Primary School. She received her bachelor of arts degree from Luther College in Decorah, Iowa, and completed her fifth year for her California teaching credential at San Diego State University. She has been a SUAVE teacher since the beginning of the program in 1994. In 1996 she became a SUAVE mentor/liaison teacher for her school. She has participated in a Fulbright grant in India, where she studied puppetry. She currently serves on the Valley Center-Pauma School district visual and performing arts committee.

**Karen Sleichter** attended California State University at Long Beach and University of California Los Angeles, where she earned a BA in English and an MA in education. She presently teaches kindergarten in the Escondido Union School District. Six years ago Karen joined the SUAVE Arts in Education program. She has presented at the California Kindergarten Conference, the Greater San Diego Math Conference, and California Association for Gifted. She was a recipient of a Fulbright grant and traveled to India to study puppetry. "Teaching through the arts makes learning come alive in the classroom." SUAVE has provided a powerful vehicle to incorporate this magic into her classroom.

**Deborah Small** received her MFA from University of California in 1983 and is a professor in the visual and performing arts program at California State University San Marcos. She is currently working on an interdisciplinary collaborative project, *Mixtec Medicine,* to explore the uses of medicinal plants by Mixtec healers in Mexico and California. She also is working on a collaboration with California State University San Marcos students and the San Luis Rey Band of Luiseño Indians on the Indian Rock/Native Plant Project, focusing on social, cultural, and botanical preservation and restoration. Her book, *Routine Contaminations,* was published in August 2002 by Cedar Hill Publications. She has received numerous awards, including two individual NEA grants and several NEA grants for collaborative work.

**Lydia Vogt** is principal of Valley Center Primary School in Valley Center, California, and current president of the California Arts Educators Association. Prior to becoming a principal, she was an elementary school teacher and arts education advocate. Lydia is a recipient of a Fulbright exchange award that enabled her to be a visiting principal in Argentina, as well as a participant in another Fulbright exchange to Veracruz, Mexico. She is also an avid bird watcher.

# SUAVE Program History

*Deborah Small, participant and photographer.*

## The Pilot Year: 1994–1995

Schools
- Central Elementary, EUSD
- Alvin Dunn Elementary, SMUSD
- Valley Center Primary, VCPUSD

Teachers:        30
Students:        825

## The Second Year: 1995–1996

Schools
- Elementary, EUSD
- Alvin Dunn Elementary, SMUSD
- Valley Center Primary, VCPUSD

Teachers:        30
Students:        825

## Highlights:

- Standardized test scores rose significantly at Central Elementary, an Escondido school site, for both English and Spanish speakers.
- The first annual "Curriculum Faire" was held on June 1, 1996 at CCAE.
- "SUAVE Case Story Collection" was published highlighting a SUAVE activity or SUAVE event.
- Teachers offered CSUSM graduate credits for their participation and granted full library privileges at CSUSM library.
- SUAVE goes on the Web with its own home page.
- Merryl Goldberg received a Scholarly Research and Creative Activity Grant through CSUSM to research the effects of SUAVE on professional development.
- A mentor teacher protocol was developed and approved by all principals to enable "graduating sites" to remain as full partners.

## The Third Year: 1996–1997

Schools:
- Felicita Elementary, EUSD
- Miller Elementary, EUSD
- Richland Elementary, SMUSD
- Valley Center Upper, VCPUSD

Mentor Schools:
- Central Elementary, EUSD
- Alvin Dunn Elementary, SMUSD
- Valley Center Primary, VCPUSD

| | |
|---|---|
| Teachers: | 52 |
| Students: | 1,430 |

## Highlights:

- Original SUAVE schools became mentor schools to maintain linkage to the program.

- SUAVE was the top-rated and top-funded program ($20,000) from the California Arts Council receiving a Local Arts Education Partnership Grant 1996–1997.
- SUAVE awarded $150,000 grant from John D. and Catherine T. MacArthur Foundation and Spencer Foundation to continue research as a Professional Development and Documentation Program.

## The Fourth Year: 1997–1998

Schools:
- Del Dios Middle School, EUSD
- Grant Middle School, EUSD
- Felicita Elementary, EUSD
- Miller Elementary, EUSD
- Rock Springs Elementary, EUSD
- Casa de Amparo, OUSD
- Richland Elementary, SMUSD
- Valley Center Upper Elementary, VCPUSD

Mentor Schools:
- Central Elementary, EUSD
- Alvin Dunn Elementary, SMUSD
- Valley Center Primary, VCPUSD

| | |
|---|---|
| Teachers: | 86 |
| Students: | 2,365 |

## Highlights:

- In November, a team of Chinese teacher educators from Hangzhou College in Hangzhou, China, including the president, an artist, and a musician visited with Merryl Goldberg, the CCAE education staff, and CSUSM research team.
- On Saturday, December 7, 1997, California School Boards Association awarded Central Elementary School the Golden Bell Award for their entry of "SUAVE: Learning Subject Matter through the Arts (An Arts Partnership)."

- The San Diego *Union/Tribune* became a sponsor of the Curriculum Faire and developed the SUAVE logo.
- SUAVE teachers had the opportunity to attend a private workshop with the world renown mime, Marcel Marceau.

## The Fifth Year: 1998–1999

Schools:
- Conway Elementary School, EUSD
- Del Dios Middle School, EUSD
- Grant Middle School, EUSD
- Juniper Elementary School, EUSD
- Lincoln Elementary School, EUSD
- L.R. Green Elementary School, EUSD
- North Broadway Elementary School, EUSD
- Pioneer Elementary School, EUSD
- Rock Springs Elementary, EUSD
- Rose Elementary, EUSD
- Casa de Amparo, OUSD
- Knob Hill Elementary, SMUSD
- Valley Center Lower Elementary, VCPUSD

Mentor Schools:
- Central Elementary, EUSD
- Felicita Elementary, EUSD
- Miller Elementary, EUSD
- Alvin Dunn Elementary, SMUSD
- Richland Elementary, SMUSD
- Valley Center Primary, VCPUSD
- Valley Center Upper Elementary, VCPUSD

Teachers:         152
Students:         4,180

### Highlights:

- On June 9, 1998, the Escondido Union School Board adopted SUAVE as their visual arts and performing arts curriculum for grades K–5 and voted unanimously to expand the SUAVE program to all elementary schools by 2002.
- CCAE hired eight arts coaches to meet the needs of the school districts.
- Free after-school workshops, "SUAVE Mondays," are offered to all teachers at every school site. These project-oriented workshops in drama, grammar, poetry, and visual arts ensured one more way for SUAVE to provide access to arts for all teachers.
- SUAVE in-service days expanded to two just to accommodate all 200 teachers.
- SUAVE art coaches, along with selected mentor teachers, received a prestigious Fulbright-Hays grant to study the art of puppetry and dance in India during December 1999. India is well known for its use of puppetry and dance in culture and in learning.

## The Sixth Year: 1999–2000

Schools:
- Conway Elementary School, EUSD
- Del Dios Middle School, EUSD
- Fallbrook High School, FUHSD
- Glen View Elementary School, EUSD
- Grant Middle School, EUSD
- Juniper Elementary School, EUSD
- Lincoln Elementary School, EUSD
- L.R. Green Elementary School, EUSD
- North Broadway Elementary School, EUSD
- Orange Glen Elementary School, EUSD
- Pioneer Elementary School, EUSD
- Rose Elementary, EUSD
- Casa de Amparo, OUSD
- Knob Hill Elementary, SMUSD
- Valley Center Lower Elementary, VCPUSD

Mentor Schools:
- Central Elementary, EUSD
- Felicita Elementary, EUSD

- Miller Elementary, EUSD
- Alvin Dunn Elementary, SMUSD
- Richland Elementary, SMUSD
- Rock Springs Elementary, EUSD
- Valley Center Primary, VCPUSD
- Valley Center Upper Elementary, VCPUSD

Teachers:            176
Students:            4,840

## Highlights:

- A great success of the SUAVE in-services was the workshop of the "Artist Showcase" that featured the arts and creative works of each of the SUAVE art coaches.
- Last year's free after-school workshops, "SUAVE Mondays," were changed to "SUAVE Tuesdays." These project-oriented workshops in drama, grammar, poetry, and visual arts ensured one more way for SUAVE to provide access to arts for all teachers.
- SUAVE art coaches and mentor teachers went to India on a prestigious Fulbright-Hays grant to study the art of puppetry from November 26 to December 22, 1999. The group returned with wonderful techniques of puppetry that were utilized throughout all school districts.
- A new program was developed, "More of the Best of SUAVE on Tour" (AKA SUAVE Expansion) providing intensive five- and eight-week visual art time travel and dance time travel workshops in Escondido, San Marcos, and VCPUSDs. These school districts received funding from the California Department of Education. The focus will concentrate on the fourth and fifth grades in the respective districts.
- "More of the Best of SUAVE on Tour" (SUAVE Expansion) received funding for a second year (2000–2001) from the California Department of Education to create intensive five- and eight-week sessions of music, photography, and theater. "SUAVE on Tour" EUSD will have the fourth grade experience a music time travel; San Marcos Unified School District fourth-grade classes will encounter a theater time travel, and Valley Center Middle School will be exposed to the photography time travel.

## The Seventh Year: 2000–2001

Schools:
- Casa de Amparo, OUSD
- Central Elementary, EUSD
- Fallbrook High School, FUHSD
- Felicita Elementary, EUSD
- Glen View Elementary, EUSD
- Grant Middle School, EUSD
- Lincoln Primary/Lincoln Intermediate, EUSD
- Miller Elementary, EUSD
- Oak Hill Elementary, EUSD
- Orange Glen Elementary, EUSD
- Valley Center Primary, VCPUSD

Mentor Schools:
- Alvin Dunn Elementary, SMUSD
- Conway Elementary, EUSD
- Juniper Elementary, EUSD
- Knob Hill Elementary, SMUSD
- L.R. Green Elementary, EUSD
- North Broadway, EUSD
- Pioneer Elementary, EUSD
- Richland Elementary, SMUSD
- Rock Springs Elementary, EUSD
- Rose Elementary, EUSD
- Valley Center Lower Elementary, VCPUSD
- Valley Center Upper Elementary, VCPUSD

Special Contract Sites:
- Boys & Girls Club, Critical Hours Program
- Escondido Christian School
- Grant Elementary, Mission Hills

Teachers            178
Students:           5,000

## Highlights:

- SUAVE mentor teachers began presenting arts integration workshops at SUAVE in-services.
- SUAVE after-school, project-oriented workshops in drama, grammar, poetry, and visual arts, held on-site at full-program schools, provided another way for district teachers to benefit from the SUAVE program.
- SUAVE expansion programs were once again in Escondido Union, San Marcos Unified, and Valley Center-Pauma Unified school districts. These school districts received funding from the California Department of Education. The SUAVE expansion focus is on fourth and fifth graders.
- SUAVE expansion received funding for a third year (2000–2001) from the California Department of Education to create all new programs. "Drama and the Cultures of California" will be experienced by all Escondido Union School District fourth graders, and "Kinesthetic Learning through Movement" will be in all Valley Center-Pauma Unified School District kindergarten classrooms.

## The Eighth Year: 2001–2002

Schools:
- Central Elementary, EUSD
- Felicita Elementary, EUSD
- Grand Middle School, EUSD
- Miller Elementary, EUSD
- Oak Hill Elementary, EUSD
- Rock Springs Elementary, EUSD
- Valley Center Lower Elementary, VCPUSD
- Valley Center Primary, VCPUSD
- Valley Center Upper Elementary, VCPUSD
- Pauma School, VCPUSD

Mentor Sites:
- Conway Elementary, EUSD
- Glen View Elementary, EUSD
- Juniper Elementary, EUSD
- Lincoln Primary, EUSD
- Lincoln Intermediate, EUSD
- L.R. Green Elementary, EUSD
- North Broadway, EUSD
- Orange Glen Elementary, EUSD
- Pioneer Elementary, EUSD
- Rose Elementary, EUSD
- Knob Hill Elementary, SMUSD

Special Contract Sites:
- Casa de Amparo
- Fallbrook High School
- CSUSM GEAR-UP at Grant Middle School

## Highlights

- SUAVE expansion programs were in Escondido and Valley Center. In Escondido, all fourth graders received "Drama and the Cultures of California," while all kindergartners in Valley Center received "Kinesthetic Learning through Movement."
- Received California Department of Education Arts Work grant for San Pasqual Union School District.
- SUAVE Arts Coaches and a number of SUAVE teachers went to Vera Cruz, Mexico, on a prestigious Fulbright scholarship. They returned with song, dance, and stories that will be implemented into their teaching.

# Index